BECOMING THE BRIDE OF CHRIST

Copyright 2022 John Burns

All rights reserved.

ISBN: 979-8-4056127-4-4

All rights reserved. Non-commercial interests may reproduce portions of this book without the express written permission of the author, provided the text does not exceed 500 words. When reproducing text from this book, include the following credit line: "Becoming The Bride of Christ by John Burns. Used by permission."

Commercial interests: No part of this publication may be reproduced in any form, stored in a retrieval system, or transmitted in any form by any means - electronic, photocopy, recording, or otherwise - without prior written permission of the publisher, except as provided by the United States of America copyright law.

BECOMING THE BRIDE OF CHRIST

A COMPREHENSIVE GUIDE TO UNDERSTANDING WHAT HAS GONE WRONG WITH CHRISTIAN WITNESS OVER THE LAST 2,000 YEARS OF CHURCH HISTORY

John Burns

Dedication

To the men of Task Force Ranger and Bravo Company 3/75 Ranger Regiment.

To Jesus Christ for saving me from myself.

Table of Contents

Dedication 4
Preface 7
Teshuva: Revival 9
Revelation 2:1-7
Unto the Angel of the Church of Ephesus 15
   The Ephesian Dilemma 15
Revelation 2:8-11
Unto the Angel of the Church of Smyrna 23
   Willingness of Smyrna 23
Revelation 2:12-17
Unto the Angel of the Church of Pergamos ... 30
   The Seat of Satan on Earth 31
   The Two-Edged Sword 36
   The Stumbling Block 41
Revelation 2:18-29
Unto the Angel of the Church of Thyatira 47
   The Church of Thyatira 48
   The Babylonian Legend 53

Table of Contents

    Works Replaced God's Grace 58

Revelation 3:1-6
Unto the Angel of the Church of Sardis 63

    The Reformation Church of Sardis 63
    Thou Hast a Name 67
    I Go to Prepare You a Place 71
    I Will Come on Thee as a Thief 76
    The Bride Veiled 80
    Joy Through Suffering 86
    A Hereditary Priesthood 91
    Thou Hast a Few Names 95
    Leviticus 25:10 100
    The Shmita 104

Revelation 3:7-13
Unto the Angel of the Church of Philadelphia 110

    The Missionary Church 111
    The Synagogue of Satan 115
    The Hour of Temptation 119

Revelation 3:14-22
Unto the Angel of the Church of Laodicea 123

    Christ's Letter to Laodicea 124
    I Hate Divorce 128
    He that Hath an Ear 132

Special Operations Wounded Warriors 138

Biography 146

Preface

Join me as we go behind the veil of eternity to adjudicate just what has gone wrong with the Church of Jesus Christ in all of its forms.

Within modern Christian circles. Church attendance has become more important than relationship to Jesus Christ the God-man. God established Old Testament patterns to teach a sinner proper relationship and where it should come from.

Levirite marriage is one of those patterns.

God has been searching the Gentile world to find his son a willing virgin bride. He has sent his Holy Spirit to request our hands in marriage. The dowry was paid on Calvary!

To enter true Christian relationship requires humility.

What has been lost is proper Hebrew interpretation techniques used by every writer of our New Testament. Anti-Semitism has led to the Church denying Messiah's inheritance of sitting upon the throne of King David for 1,000 years. Amillennialism denies Messiah his reward of a virgin bride promised by God from eternity past.

Preface

Jesus Christ preached only out of the Old Testament. He wrote our entire Bible before he spoke our universe into existence. All for the purpose of proving God is in charge of every affair of men. You can find yourself in the lives of Old Testament characters. None more important than the Gentile brides grafted into the Jewish vine as examples for us today.

Jesus Christ penned seven letters to seven Churches founded by John in Western Turkey. Why these seven?

This book explains what exactly happened to men calling themselves Christian over the last 2,000 years. Messiah's letters were a prophetic view on just how far church folk have gotten away from the truth of God's entire two-edged sword.

Mercy and grace are what Messiah offered on Calvary. He still offers his body the same attributes he first offered the apostles when he called them in antiquity.

He was crucified upon a cross of wood, yet he created the hill upon which it stood.

He is alive forevermore and he is returning for his true virgin bride very soon!

Teshuva: Revival

When I pass a denominational church in America, and see the word revival, it causes me to pose the question? What does the word revival mean?

Using proper Hebrew hermeneutics, the Biblical Hebrew word found in the Old Testament is the word "Chayah." The transliteration to English in our King James Bible is where we glean the word revival. The Hebrew definition by which we are to experience revival is rooted in bringing something back to life. To restore to consciousness or to restore to a previous condition.

Using only Jesus Christ's Biblical model, revival is grounded in a personal return to the word of God after asking God for mercy. Why does mercy precede revival? Mercy is the foundation upon which God is building the tabernacle of grace in the lives of individual believers. Your spiritual house of grace can only be built upon God's foundation of eternal mercy. Mercy is gleaned only when we study God's interaction with the stiff-necked people God is married to forever. They are our Jewish ancestors found in the pages of our Old Testament.

When mercy had been exhausted in the lives of the nation God birthed in Egypt, Israel, grace appeared in Jerusalem. Grace has a name. It is Yeshua ha Messiach or in English: Jesus Christ. Jesus Christ himself said he came unto the lost sheep of Israel, to save them from their sins. They were to become the first Christian witnesses to the world that had fallen so far away from worship of the world's creator. The first apostles were Jewish. The first Christian martyrs, were Jewish. The 120 disciples in the upper room on Pentecost were Jewish. The Jewish men Christ called to witness of his death, burial, and resurrection were all Jewish. Salvation has always been of the Jew first and then the Greek. I am the Lord and, I change not. Hallelujah!

Mercy is to not receive what we all deserve; for the wages of sin is death, but the gift of God is eternal life through Jesus Christ our Lord. A Christian that is alive today, requires the same mercy they received at the point of accepting Jesus Christ's entire testimony of himself. This is called justification. Paul begins to illuminate who the just are in the book of Galatians. Justification is a legal term applied by Paul to describe what happens when a sinner accepts God's propitiation for sin Jesus Christ's death removed the penalty of sin over our lives. No double jeopardy in God's world. Forgiven and never to be tried again for our sins. Jesus Christ's death, for our eternal life. Our freedom for his imprisonment. Our Joy for his grief. And he did it all because he loves you, even if you were the only one. Hallelujah!

Mercy in the life of a Christian that produces God's justification, is the foundation for Christian revival. However, justification is only the first step in our Christian walk. There are two other steps taught by Paul to the Jewish and Gentile world that Christ entered. Justification should lead a believer to understand that we exist in the presence of sin. It is the power of sin that Christians will wrestle with, until Messiah returns. Until we are removed from the presence of sin, mercy should be our prayer so grace can appear in our lives. Grace is imputed to us sinners, only when we have the continuous humility to ask for God's eternal mercy. Hallelujah!

Sanctification is God's offer to Christians to overcome the power of sin in our lives. Sanctification is a continuous process that begins when we open the Bible and study to show ourselves approved, a workman rightly dividing the word of truth. It is an individual effort. Revival can only begin, when individual Christians pray to God. Open the Bible daily to see if what John Burns is saying is true. And a Christian testifies as to the overcoming nature of our most Holy Spirit in our own lives, with those we come into contact with daily. Who is an overcomer? 1 John 5:4. One who believes in the death, burial, and resurrection of Jesus Christ. A sanctified sinner is one who looks in the mirror, and judges only themselves by what the Bible says. Jesus Christ died to raise dead men to life. He did not die to make bad men good, for all the thoughts of man is only evil continually. To overcome evil in my own life, nothing but a return to thus says the Lord will suffice. To know evil from God's point of view takes the utmost humility. It is not the evil western educated seminary pastors' prostitute in their houses of worship every Sunday and Wednesday evening. God does not dwell in houses made with human hands. His desire has always been to inhabit the tabernacle of every person born of a woman. Corporate revival in church will only begin with individuals returning to the entire testimony of God found in both testaments of our most Holy Bible. Hallelujah!

Paul reminds us in Romans that the just shall live by faith. Romans 1:17 is the beginning of Paul teaching us what the product of justification in the lives of the sinner is. Faith is justification's only reward. Justification produced persecution in the lives of the people Christ convinced of his nature as God. Is it any different today? Should Christianity be comfortable? I think not. Teshuva. Repent and return to the word of God in your individual life, persecution will follow, but take heart, for Christ has overcome the world once and for all. Revival will begin in America and in American denominational churches only when we return to God's entire testimony of his entire written word.

Sanctification is the second step for professing Christians that will one day lead to the promise of God of eternal life. Glorification is the third step in our Christian walk. It is our removal from the presence of sin. It occurs either at the point of physical death, or in my life, it will occur when God removes me from the wrath to come before the tribulation of the last seven years of Gentile government on earth. It is the period of time, revealed by Daniel as the 70th week of Israel's trials. It is referred to in the bible as the time of Jacob's troubles. The Holocaust will look like a picnic, when the Satanic trinity begins to persecute God's people in America. The Jewish remnant God removed from European persecution, has a short time to return to Israel as God commanded. Soon the man of lawlessness will be revealed, the bride will be removed, and Church goers will fall away completely from Jesus Christ's true doctrines found in the pages of the Old Testament. Our blessed hope as professing Christians should be the doctrine of the rapture taught by Enoch, Elijah, Rahab the harlot, Jesus Christ in John 14, and Paul the Apostle in the books referred to as his letter to the Thessalonians.

Jesus Christ dictated 7 letters to seven churches in the book of Revelation. Of those seven churches only two are removed prior to the tribulation. Smyrna and Philadelphia. Smyrna is the persecuted Church. Those rare individuals willing to die for the testimony of Jesus Christ. Philadelphia being the missionary church who constantly witnesses to our fallen world while not being infected by church and men's traditions. The message of our gospel was intended for every person born of a woman and God needs individual Christian witness outside of the confines of church. Every person, every day, all the time. That is the church of Philadelphia. Sanctified by the entire word of God, and willing to die for their testimony! Hallelujah!

Jesus Christ used a peculiar Greek word to describe the period of time between the church age and the tribulation of the last days. The word Meta-tauta is the final admonition to the church of Laodicea and it is the first word in Revelation 4. It means after these things. In Laodicea, the Churches are on Earth. In chapter 4 verse 1, the command to come up here and I will show which things shall be hereafter is a reference to the rapture. The true Church is in Heaven in chapter four of the book of Revelation. God always removes the righteous before he brings the vengeance of his wrath upon the earth. The bride of Christ is a subset of the body of Christ. Not all of the body of Christ will be raptured. Settle it in your heart this day whether Jesus Christ is indeed the Lord of your life? If you make Christ the Lord of your life, he must become your bridegroom and you must become his willing virgin bride. <u>You must forgo church tradition in favor of thus says the Lord.</u> When you do, your life will never be the same. Ask yourself a question? Would God spend 2,000 years and counting, finding his son a bride, only to beat her up for seven years? Not my God. Not my Jesus! He loves us and he is presently building my mansion in Heaven. He will very soon remove me from the wrath that is fast approaching the America that I love. Teshuva. Repent and return to the Bible today.

No privilege have I enjoyed more, than the privilege God gave me when he began to take me behind the veil of eternity 28 years ago. I have rebelled so many times, but God alone pre-destined me for salvation, marriage to his son, co-ruling on earth with Jesus Christ from Jerusalem, upon completion of the tribulation. 1,000 years, I will be by Jesus Christ side as one of the 24 priest Kings worshipping at the altar of God in heaven. Ruling and reigning over all the kingdoms of this world with my risen Jewish Messiah, the Lord Jesus Christ. Choose this day whom you will serve, as for me and my house, we will serve the Lord.

He was crucified upon a cross of wood, yet he created the hill upon which it stood.

John Burns 6-27-2021.

Revelation 2:1-7 Unto the Angel of the Church of Ephesus

2 Unto the angel of the church of Ephesus write; These things saith he that holdeth the seven stars in his right hand, who walketh in the midst of the seven golden candlesticks; ² I know thy works, and thy labour, and thy patience, and how thou canst not bear them which are evil: and thou hast tried them which say they are apostles, and are not, and hast found them liars: ³ And hast borne, and hast patience, and for my name's sake hast laboured, and hast not fainted. ⁴ Nevertheless I have somewhat against thee, because thou hast left thy first love. ⁵ Remember therefore from whence thou art fallen, and repent, and do the first works; or else I will come unto thee quickly, and will remove thy candlestick out of his place, except thou repent. ⁶ But this thou hast, that thou hatest the deeds of the Nicolaitanes, which I also hate. ⁷ He that hath an ear, let him hear what the Spirit saith unto the churches; To him that overcometh will I give to eat of the tree of life, which is in the midst of the paradise of God.

The Ephesian Dilemma

The Ephesian Church is one of the two churches to have two letters addressed to it. The first by Paul the Apostle to the

Gentiles and the letter Jesus Christ dictated to the church's founder, and writer of the book of Revelation, one of the sons of thunder, John the Apostle.

We will begin our study with the letter Jesus Christ dictated to an Angel to be delivered and written by John. The seven letters to the seven churches, are the most important teachings a member of God's kingdom can rightly divide.

The word Revelation is singular not plural. It is one revelation of Jesus Christ's true church, as labeled by Messiah as his bride. He being masculine, the word Ephesus is a feminine pronoun. It is understood as "My desired one." It is the Apostolic Church founded by John and admonished by Jesus Christ and Paul.

Ephesus is a city on the coast of western Turkey in modern Izmir province. It enjoyed a geographic position as the center of Pagan Greek worship. The Temple of Artemis was in Ephesus. Greek life revolved around the veneration of created deities. Ephesus is the feminine goddess of fertility. Her roots can be traced to the cult of Semiramis in Babylon. She is most often depicted posing with reindeer, for she is the deity Americans call mother nature. John the Apostle set up shop in Ephesus after escaping persecution in Jerusalem.

Ephesus was first settled by the Lydian Greek colonists in the 14th and 13th centuries, BC. It is where Greek life was full. There was a theatre, a gymnasium, a massive library, and the Temple of Artemis. It was considered the most modern city of it's time. Greek life in western Turkey was centered in Ephesus for a long time. It would be conquered by Cyrus the great who allowed for the worship of Artemis to continue. It would be re-conquered by Alexander the Great and Hellenization took on renewed life as he funded the construction of the city. At the time of John and Paul, Ephesus was the center of Roman life in western Turkey.

The ancient Jewish people had settled in Ephesus and at the time of the Apostles, there was a prominent Jewish synagogue in the city center. This is a paradigm of our Jewish ancestor's fate as God chose to destroy their temple in Jerusalem, and send them packing around the entire globe. The diaspora begun in 70 AD is drawing to a close as I pen these words. Israel is in the land and prospering, America finds itself under the abandonment wrath of Yeshua, and the Laodicean Church has manifest around the globe. Where the carcasses lie, there the eagles shall be gathered.

Paul the Apostle, lays the groundwork for the admonishment Jesus Christ would issue in Revelation 2. Ephesians 3;18 is Paul's remedy for the problem they had. Paul tells the church to allow their whole breadth, width, depth and height to be sanctified to the will of God the father. The Church of Ephesus was only getting three of them right.

Depth, width, and height are easy for most professing Christians to sanctify. It is church attendance and ministry outreach. But what about breadth?

The word breadth in the original koine Greek translation was understood as a great expanse of time. To cross the breadth of the ocean requires a sea captain to spend a lot of time learning to navigate the entire breadth of the ocean expanse.

Breadth to the Greek mind, has nothing to do with church, it has everything to do with how much time you spend alone with Jesus Christ.

Paul the Apostle laid out in Ephesians what God sees as true membership in his kingdom of Jew and Greek peoples. John was reminded to issue the rebuke for what they were getting wrong. The Ephesian church was going to church every week. They chose the Roman model for worship on the venerable day of the Sun. Sunday. God's sabbath will always be Shabbat. Friday evening to Saturday evening. It is one of two days that Jesus Christ will be in the temple during the millennium. The other is the new moon. Sunday is the day the Roman Caesars gave slaves the day off. Six days shall a man work and on the seventh he shall rest. Sunday is the first day of the work week in God's Bible. It has never changed. Men changed in their haste to assimilate to Roman, Pagan traditions.

Ephesus is where many Pagan traditions migrated into church worship services. Roman holidays began to be venerated by Ephesian Christians, and time spent earning income became more important than spending time with Jesus Christ. Alone in prayer and supplication with thanksgiving. And in the sanctifying work of the study of scripture. This is why there is absolutely no power in the Gospel being taught in today's denominational churches. They are ok with Roman holidays and church tradition started by our ancestors. They are fine with lukewarm Christianity.

Jesus Christ admonished the Ephesian church with the words "YOU have lost your first Love". He was speaking to John the revelator and an amazing recipient of the love of Christ. It is John who introduces the world to the agape love of Jesus Christ. It is John who was entrusted with the care of Jesus Christ's mother Mary. She is buried in Ephesus right beside John the Apostle today.

Since Jesus Christ saw fit to entrust John with the care of his mother, and the admonition of the Church, he must also be the one who can provide Christians with the remedy to our dilemma.

1 John 5:4,5 is the remedy for those who have an ear to hear. Do you have an ear to hear what the Spirit is saying to the modern Ephesian Church? For whatsoever is born of God overcometh the world: and this is the victory that overcometh the world, even our faith. Who is he that overcometh the world but he that believes Jesus Christ is the Son of God. Hallelujah!

The Ephesian letter is a letter that should give us Biblical hope. It was at Ephesus that Christ introduces us to the prophetic timeline of church history. Ephesus denotes the Apostolic Church age. It begins with the calling of the twelve and ends with the martyrdom of Polycarp in Smyrna. He is the bishop John anoints at Ephesus to be over the Church of Smyrna and the second church Jesus Christ addresses in his letters to the seven Churches. Smyrna is the place where Gentile persecution begins to occur in western Turkey.

Revelation 2:1-7 Unto the Angel of the Church of Ephesus

The Ephesian letter finishes with the practical application of Christian faith. We are commanded to put on the full armor of God. Having our loins girt about with truth, having on the breastplate of righteousness, our feet shod with the preparation of the gospel of peace, taking the shield of faith, the helmet of salvation, and the sword of the spirit which is the word of God.

At the time of the writing of Paul's admonition to the Ephesian Church, Rome was the world superpower. The sword the Roman legionnaire would take into battle was the two-edged gladius. Our Bible is one message with two edges over two testaments. Mercy is the message of the Old Testament, and grace is who appears in the New Testament. He has a name. It is Yeshua ha Messiah or Jesus Christ in English. He preached salvation from a Hebrew hermeneutical perspective gleaned while he was writing the Old Testament in eternity past. He is the author and finisher of our faith. He is the Lion of the tribe of Judah. He is the Alpha and the Omega; he is the Aleph and the Tau. He is our redeemer. He is coming soon at the sound of the trumpet to retrieve his bride and bring her to heaven to receive her mansion. He will return to this world with his bride at the end of the tribulation to receive his kingdom and inheritance. He is alive forever more. Hallelujah!

The Ephesian Church had become so adept at church attendance once or twice a week, they were now ok with not spending time with Messiah. John could not wait to see Christ in the Gospel period. After the resurrection, church attendance became more important than personal relationship to Jesus Christ. It was comfortable having people see you at church. Outward piety, replaced inward conviction. Jesus Christ is upset.

The one thing the Ephesians were getting ~~write~~ right was that they hated any type of church hierarchy. Relationship to God was personal. The Nicolaitans were the precursors to the Pope, bishops, priests, deacons, and lay people who started a government where men lorded over the lives of believers. It was a cult started by the deacon Nicholas in Acts 6. The words can be derived from two Greek words. Nicao: to rule over, and Laity: the people. There is one mediator between God and man, the Lord Jesus Christ. Jesus Christ hates any type of church hierarchy where men set up other men who appear outwardly pious but inside, they are ravenous wolves. The only person to earn a wage from Christ's crucifixion and the Gospel was Judas! Christ condemned the need for government in church.

The reaction of the Roman government was to begin wholesale persecution of Gentile Christians in Asia minor beginning with the martyrdom of Polycarp. It would not end until Constantine married government to the Christian Church at Pergamos. Persecution was the lot for professing Christians from Stephen through the current persecution of believers in Africa and other countries where government as God leaves believers in Christ with no other option than death. Are you willing to die for Christ testimony of himself? If not, then you are not justified or should I say, saved.

Even so come Lord Jesus Christ. He was crucified upon a cross of wood, yet he created the hill upon which it stood.

John Burns 6-28-2021.

Revelation 2:8-11 Unto the Angel of the Church of Smyrna

8 And unto the angel of the church in Smyrna write; These things saith the first and the last, which was dead, and is alive; ⁹ I know thy works, and tribulation, and poverty, (but thou art rich) and I know the blasphemy of them which say they are Jews, and are not, but are the synagogue of Satan. ¹⁰ Fear none of those things which thou shalt suffer: behold, the devil shall cast some of you into prison, that ye may be tried; and ye shall have tribulation ten days: be thou faithful unto death, and I will give thee a crown of life. ¹¹ He that hath an ear, let him hear what the Spirit saith unto the churches; He that overcometh shall not be hurt of the second death.

Willingness of Smyrna

Jesus Christ addressed the Church of Smyrna, having endured the humiliation of the Roman execution at the hands of the Jewish high priest. God was dealing the death blow to human religion in any form. The Church of Smyrna is the shining example of when a Christian knows they are saved.

Revelation 2:8-11 Unto the Angel of the Church of Smyrna

Smyrna is a feminine pronoun. It comes from the root word Myrrh. This is one of the three gifts brought to Mary and Joseph by the Magi from Persia. It is a spice used for the Jewish burial right. It is a gift most often presented to Kings. Jesus Christ is the world's messiah who will one day receive a kingdom in Jerusalem at the end of the times of Jacob's trials. It is Jesus Christ inheritance promised to his mother Mary, while he was yet in her womb.

The church of Smyrna should be what every Christian is willing to endure, persecution to the point of death. This is how a Christian knows they are saved. A willingness to lay down your life for the testimony that Jesus Christ is the God of mercy and grace. He died to pay the only debt that matters when you die. Your sin debt to God the father.

Human religion had taken hold in Ephesus. God's reaction, was to convict Gentile Christians that they must be willing to die to dogma and doctrine, in favor of dying for Christ in the flesh. Smyrna is where it all began for Gentiles. Polycarp is the first gentile martyr and the last eyewitness to the ministry of the Apostle whom Jesus Loved. John anointed Polycarp to be the Bishop of Smyrna. He would be burnt at the stake and eventually run through with a Roman spear to finish his execution at the hands of the Roman pro-consulate in Smyrna. Rome feared insurrection, Christianity was at odds with the accepted Roman pantheon to include Caesar worship. It is no different in America today. God has not changed.

We are living in the times the Bible has a lot to say about. Yet we cling to our denominational structures and Church liturgy to our own peril. God has been building a kingdom of Jew and Gentile, while we build A-Millenial houses of worship, where God is not present. Smyrna is one of the two Church's Jesus Christ had nothing bad to say about. Philadelphia is the second. Choose this day whom you will serve. As for me and my house, we will serve the Lord.

A willingness to die for what Jesus Christ taught began for Gentile's at Smyrna. John the revelator had begun to preach Christ death, burial, and resurrection in Smyrna. It was a Greek colony where Rome had begun to assert its' fledgling power in western Turkey. Caesar worship was the center of Roman life. Pontifex Maximus was the religious title Augustus had chosen for himself, following the Babylonian pantheon that emigrated to Western Turkey from the banks of the Euphrates. His power was absolute, and any religion that challenged his authority was squashed, and martyrdom was the choice of the fledgling gentile converts to Christianity in Smyrna.

Smyrna was located at the confluence of two rivers that emptied into the Aegean Sea. This location led the Ionian colonists to build elaborate Temples to the River God Kaestros. Smyrna was considered a colony of Ephesus and Artemis was one of the early goddesses venerated by the Greek colonists. Smyrna was conquered and re-conquered many times during its' ancient history. Alexander the Great rebuilt the city, and his Generals fought for control of Smyrna until the times of the Roman colonization.

Smyrna was a strategic port city. Commerce flowed through frequently and was distributed throughout the Aeolian peninsula. Religion dominated the lives of the people who lived in ancient Smyrna. When the Romans began to dominate the region, they melded the Greek pantheon with their Roman Caesar worship. Roman mythology emanated from Greek settlers of the Italian peninsula. They enjoyed the same founding myths* the Aeolian Greeks identified with. Rome repackaged the Babylonian gods and goddesses as a part of asserting their will on the lives of the people they conquered. As a colony of Ephesus, Artemis was the principal goddess born to Zeus venerated by the Greeks at Smyrna.

Smyrna according to Christ begins the times of Gentile persecution for our testimony. No greater love hath a man than this, that he lay down his life for his friends. This is Jesus Christ model for true Christian worship. It is this pattern that has been resurrected in these last days. Men and women willing to forgo the worship of America's gods, and be persecuted to the point of death by those unwilling to believe in Christ. Death to one self has always been at the heart of Christian testimony. Understanding what that means, is at the heart of individual Christian conviction. Individual conviction, is how God has been building Christ kingdom.

The church of Smyrna was an underground church. It occurred in people's houses, not in three- dimensional church structures. Temple's, have always made God angry. The tabernacle God desires to inhabit, is the three -part temple known as the human condition. Spirit, soul, and body, individually sanctified to the will of God the father in heaven. God does not dwell in houses made with human hands. His desire is to inhabit your entire existence all the time. He loves you, and he laid down his life for you on a wooden cross at a place called Calvary. The nails did not hold him to the cross, his love for you and me held him there! Hallelujah.

Smyrna was the church that was actually practicing Johns' message of overcoming taught by John in his first letter. 1John 5;4 is the key to becoming an overcomer. Believing that Jesus Christ as God manifest in the flesh is the foundation for Christian testimony. God became the son of God in the womb of Mary. To divide Jesus Christ divinity from his humanity is called Synecretism. The melding of two belief systems to appease government as God, was not the testimony of the church of Smyrna. They overcame to the point of death by understanding that it was God on that cross. It was God who left eternity past, present and future, to enter our dimension of time, and die a humiliating death at the hands of those he LOVED forever! Hallelujah.

Smyrna followed the biblical pattern of willingness to die for God's perfect will for our lives. Fear can never be the testimony of Christians. Fear is the opposite of faith. Faith is the substance of things hoped for, the evidence of things not seen. It is completely a production of God's Holy Spirit. Faith is a gift from God. It is not something you do it must become who you are. For faith to truly activate, the willingness to die to all religious pre-suppositions must be at the heart of your

Christian testimony, holding on will never lead to letting go! God is the God of surrender. He surrendered to the Jewish high priest willingly. He surrendered to Pilates' verdict and never opened his mouth to defend the indefensible. He surrendered to the grave knowing it was a temporary existence. Have you surrendered to God as Messiah over your entire life? What could you possibly hold onto? God let it all go on the cross. Hallelujah.

This message is a prophetic warning from behind the veil of eternity. The letters to the seven Church's, are Jesus Christ prophetic warning to his bride, and my message continues the pattern begun by Christ in western Turkey. To become the bride of Christ is to unlock the secrets of the word of God.it is the true blessed hope God established during his ministry to his creation in Jerusalem. He came to the lost sheep of Israel who were practicing human religion. Their fate is temporary. Gentile salvation was first offered by Paul in Antioch. It migrated to the Jewish synagogues in western Turkey. Upon John's release from Patmos, Christ instructed him to enter the homes of people to include Gentile's living in the incredibly Greek Pagan world of Ionia. Patmos is where gentile Christianity became real. To die for the testimony of Christ is the responsibility of all who claim faith in Yeshua ha Messiah.

I am a Smyrnian, Philadelphia Christian. I am willing to lay down my life for the testimony of Christ any- time, anywhere. This belief requires that I go ye into all the world and preach Christ and Paul's Gospel. It is all centered in God's preposterous debt payment plan. He created us with the inherent ability to deny him as our creator. Because he is a God who can- not learn and he can- not lie, he had to pay our debt himself to deliver us from the fear of dying to one's self. Salvation must begin between your own ear's. The distance between your ears is the greatest gulf God intends to breach with the message of the Gospel. Choose this day whom you will truly serve. Serve Christ with the willingness to die to self and endure persecution, or serve at the houses of worship where God is not present.

He was crucified upon a cross of wood, yet he created the hill upon which it stood.

Even so come Lord Jesus Christ.

John Burns 7-4-2021.

Revelation 2:12-17 Unto the Angel of the Church of Pergamos

12 And to the angel of the church in Pergamos write; These things saith he which hath the sharp sword with two edges; ¹³ I know thy works, and where thou dwellest, even where Satan's seat is: and thou holdest fast my name, and hast not denied my faith, even in those days wherein Antipas was my faithful martyr, who was slain among you, where Satan dwelleth. ¹⁴ But I have a few things against thee, because thou hast there them that hold the doctrine of Balaam, who taught Balac to cast a stumblingblock before the children of Israel, to eat things sacrificed unto idols, and to commit fornication. ¹⁵ So hast thou also them that hold the doctrine of the Nicolaitanes, which thing I hate. ¹⁶ Repent; or else I will come unto thee quickly, and will fight against them with the sword of my mouth. ¹⁷ He that hath an ear, let him hear what the Spirit saith unto the churches; To him that overcometh will I give to eat of the hidden manna, and will give him a white stone, and in the stone a new name written, which no man knoweth saving he that receiveth it.

The Seat of Satan on Earth

Jesus Christ dictated seven letters to seven churches in the book of Revelation. Revelation is the Greek word apokolupsis or unveiling. The Lord was unveiling his bride amongst the body of Christ. Pergamos is the third church Jesus Christ addressed.

Pergamos is made from two Greek words. Per meaning unholy and gamos denoting a marriage. Pergamos was the reaction of Christians to survive Roman persecution. Pergamos is the church where Constantine married the Roman solar pantheon with western Christianity. It is where Roman paganism migrated into the Christian gospel and the marriage of church and state was consummated.

Pergamos is referred to by Jesus as the seat of Satan on Earth. Why?

The Greek city of Pergamos is where Zeus was believed to have been born. A 125' by 125' bronze altar was constructed at Pergamos for the worship of Zeus. The altar was superheated, and women throughout the known world would throw their infant children on this altar to win favor with the god of war, Zeus. This is where the seeds of abortion were sown in western Christianity. When enough babies were sacrificed, Zeus was said to have been born at Pergamos.

Christians at Pergamos compromised with the Greek gods and allowed Greek Gnosticism to creep into their gospel message. Nicholas, the deacon of Colllose, mixed Greek knowledge with Christ's message. He can be found in the book of Acts chapter 6 as a deacon chosen by the apostles to take God's message to all of the known Roman-Greek world. He was to take Christ's good news to western Turkey.

He compromised with the world that then was. Beginning in Genesis 2:24, God started the paradigm by which He views His entire creation. The pattern is one where a loving God created four things. He created the heavens and the earth perfect. This is verified in Jeremiah 4:23. There are three heavens in scripture. The present heaven where God is present. The heaven above the terra firma, made up mostly of the cosmos, and our atmosphere. And the new heaven which will appear at the end of the millennium of Christ's reign on earth.

God created angels. Amongst those angels were three archangels. Lucifer, God's worship leader. Michael, God's warrior angel protecting His people Israel and Gabriel, God's messenger angel to His creation.

According to Genesis 2, something occurred between the beginning and day one of creation. That something, was a rebellion in Heaven, led by Lucifer, where he convinced one-third of the angels to worship him. Jesus Christ said he saw Lucifer fall from heaven like lightning. This rebellion caused God to flood the original creation he had created perfect. The earth had to be created again, and this time to receive God's replacement for lucifer, man.

God established the wedding covenant between one man and one woman for life as a pattern of how He views His creation. That is why God's greatest jealousy is as Creator. If you want to fall out of favor with God, worship His creation more than worship Him. God is eternally married to His creation. He does not need help saving His planet. He holds the creation in the palm of His righteous right hand. If the globe is warming, it is because God is getting ready to judge those who deny Him as creator.

Lucifer's rebellion set in motion a series of events that led to the second flood. Lucifer commanded the fallen angels, to begin having intercourse with the daughters of Adam. God found Himself a man perfect in his generation whose daughters had not polluted themselves with fallen angels. The daughters who did, produced male offspring who came to be known as the Nephillim. They had dual DNA. The purpose of the flood of Noah was to destroy the Nephillim, and re-establish the covenant God had brokered with Himself when Adam and Eve transgressed. The Messiah would be born to an unpolluted bloodline.

When Noah settled in the fertile plains of Mesopotamia, men rebelled once again, and I believe some fallen angels had escaped the judgement of the second flood, to begin leading men down an immoral ungodly path. I believe Nimrod and his wife Semiramis, were the leaders who began to replace creator worship with worship of the creation at Babel. Their rebellion has led to the formation of ancient creation worship cults, and they permeated the lives of Greek Christians in Pergamos. The unholy marriage of Christianity to fertility cults begun at Babel, migrated to western Turkey, and Jesus Christ says that is where the seat of Satan on Earth was established. He had a new throne for men to worship him on, and it was being addressed by our Messiah as one of his Churches.

The Greek colonists had settled Pergamos sometime in the 14th century BC. The temple of Pergamos was built for the purpose of human sacrifice. Specifically infant sacrifice. The marriage covenant between one man and one woman for life, was nullified. The Greeks became devoutly against monogamy and human sexuality and intercourse began to be accepted outside of the confines of the marriage covenant established by God when he made Eve to be the suitable helpmeet by which Messiah would eventually be born. Divorce in today's modern church experience has reached epidemic proportion and God is not at all happy. Repent and return to Biblical morality and sanity in all things dealing with human intercourse. Train up a child in the way they should go and when they are old, they will not depart from it.

Pergamos is where the great practitioners of all things medical got their start. Aescalepius got his start at Pergamos. He is considered the father of medicine. His symbol is the serpent on a brass pole. No doubt stolen from God. This was the same serpent on a pole that Moses was commanded to erect to heal the Israelites of bites from serpents. Aescalepius was the first in history to purvey in Pharmakia from where we get the term pharmacy. He first produced the stronghold of addiction in antiquity, and he is the reason America is the leading consumer of all things narcotic. Are you in church on Sunday and then hopelessly addicted to all things the cult of Aescalepius will provide you with on Shabbat through Shabbat?

Doctors in America attend western Greek universities, receive PHDs, become practitioners of all things Pharmakia, and Christians compromise with the word of God and Christ receiving 40-1 lashes for the healing of the flesh. There is no coincidence that Moses warned us of the 39 diseases that would befall mankind as a result of rebellion. Choose this day whom you will serve, as for me and my house we will serve the Lord. I believe Christ received the Roman lashes for the healing of the flesh. No need for the cult of Aescalepius in my life.

Gnosticism begun by Nicholas has led to American Christians worshipping Zues, Aescalepius, Artemis, Eros, astrology and every other perversion of monotheism in their haste to assimilate with the extremely pagan world we live in. Compromise with thus says the Lord from the beginning has always been man's lot in life. John the Apostle provides our means by which we can become overcomers in this life.

1 john 5:4 Believe that Jesus Christ has come in the flesh. Believe He died to pay the only debt that matters when you die: your sin debt to God as creator. Get under the blood of the Lamb, pray earnestly for the healing of your flesh. Become a Berean Christian and study scripture daily to find out if what John Burns is saying is true. Be prepared to always share the reason for the joy that is within you. He has a name. To the Jew He is Yeshua ha Messiah. To western Christians He is Jesus the Christ.

He desires to give you a white stone with a new name on it. This follows the pattern of the Romans who gave the slaves in the empire a white stone with a Latin name denoting they were eligible to enter the colosseum and watch the gladiator games. The name Jesus Christ alone knows you by, is your reward for faithful belief in His death, burial, and resurrection. This new white stone allows for your entrance into His eternal Kingdom.

One day we will rule and reign with Him over all the kingdoms of the earth. I will receive the crowns He has prepared for me in eternity past. We will be priest-kings for all eternity.

Even so come Lord Jesus Christ. He was crucified upon a cross of wood, yet he created the hill upon which it stood!

RLTW John Burns 7-11-2021.

The Two-Edged Sword

Revelation 2 provides insight into how Jesus Christ viewed God's word. It is he who said I have the sharp sword with two edges. It was Paul in Ephesians who reminds us to take with us the sword of the spirit which is the word of God. Has Jesus's opinion ever changed as to the written revealed word?

What happened to the scripture that Paul gleaned his Gospel from in 1 Corinthians 15 Vs. 1-5? I believe Christian men became devoutly antisemitic to escape persecution. I believe they began to combine Greek Gnosticism with the Roman fertility pantheon first begun in Babylon under Nimrod. The rebellion by Romanized Christian preachers was a reaction begun in Pergamos when men married Christianity to the eugenic Greek mind in western Turkey. Their goal was to secure a hierarchy of elite preachers who held a monopoly on what God thinks. They were racist then, and they are racist now. How you treat one Jewish king and his brethren in the flesh, determines whether you are saved, sanctified, and eventually glorified in the coming kingdom of Yeshua ha Messiah.

Paul was raised in Tarsus, a Roman province in an extremely pagan Greek world. The Greeks were the original purveyors of the need for socio-political elite priests who controlled the flow of information about their gods, to the common Greek citizens. To the Lord and to Christians, these men were the Nicaolaitans that Jesus Christ says he hates. They do what is right in their own eyes, and they lead people down the wide road that will lead to their eventual destruction.

The Nicaolaitans are a sect of confessing Christians who combined the Greek pantheon of gods with a little bit of New Testament Jesus. At Pergamos they allowed the worship of Ishtar to replace God's calendar established in the Old Testament. They replaced the 14th of Nisan as the date of the crucifixion, with a Roman calendar date of a Friday crucifixion. No way to get to Jesus Christ's prophecy of being in the grave three days and three nights with a Friday crucifixion.

They replaced the resurrection, with the celebration of the bunny rabbit fertility goddess Ishtar. They gave it a Roman name: Easter. The golden egg of Ashtarte had migrated into church and God is angry.

The resurrection occurred on the 17th of Nisan. Yet Christians blindly do what the men Jesus Christ hates continue to do. Make God a liar. They do not read the Bible themselves and they rely on Greek educated pastors to wrongly divide the word of truth. To divide something, you need two things which God gave all of us. The Old and New Testaments. Yet, antisemitic men and women continue to lean only on New Testament grace, without going through Old Testament mercy. Blasphemy.

The word Nicaolaitans can be understood by its English transliteration. It is gleaned from two Greek words. Nicao; To rule over and laity; The people. Jesus Christ hates any kind of church hierarchy. Period. He is the only mediator between God and men. He is the author and finisher of our faith. The anointing we receive from him is real not counterfeit, you do not need any man to teach you. The Holy Spirit was given at Christ's ascension for the purpose of finding Christ a willing bride taken from men. One person and one confession of faith at a time. The church has become a socialist mechanism for keeping government from persecuting people. 1 John 5:4 and a move away from church attendance toward home groups for worshipping is the goal of Jesus Christ. That is where Paul, Peter, Jude, John, Matthew, Mark, Luke, Titus, and James the Just, met with Christians. God does not dwell in houses made with human hands. He is the God of time while occupying all space.

Modern Christian preachers shame people into a false sense of salvation. This has been the pattern since Constantine first Romanized Christianity in 323 AD. Modern denominational

Christians deny the Gospel to most of our sinful society. They kidnap God for set periods of time, judge others while never looking into the mirror to admit they have played a role in America's abandonment wrath of God. They prostitute grace and never practice mercy. They believe God saved them to be societies judge of all things dealing with outward piety. They have no power and Jesus Christ is no-where near their three-dimensional Pagan temples. Jesus Christ is standing at the door of their Churches and knocking, which means he is outside.

Fear is the opposite of faith. Modern preachers keep their congregations in a constant state of fear because they are being paid to enlighten men to the marriage of church and state. They have no idea who Jesus Christ is according to the Old Testament. If they read the Old Testament, revival would never be needed for they would understand God would never build a house on any other foundation then those found in the Old Testament.

Modern preachers in America deny the irrevocable covenants found in our Old Testament. Genesis 12 promises how a believer can be blessed in God's eternal kingdom. Genesis 22 is the akedah and the means by which God said he would be the Lamb slain on Calvary. 2 Samuel 7:14 brings a believer behind the veil of eternity to explain that one day Jesus Christ would become the root and the offspring of King David. It is a future kingdom of Jew and Gentile to be established after the final 7 years of Gentile government on Earth. Jeremiah 31:31 is the eternal covenant that explains how God always intended to pay the sin debt of humanity by Jesus Christ. Without the knowledge of these covenants the New Testament is alone and it leads to wielding only one edge of the sword of the spirit, denying Christ's true identity and leading to Christian confusion and a lack of power in their testimony.

Mercy is the story of the Old Testament in the lives of our Jewish ancestors. Grace is the revelation of Messiah with the continuation of monotheistic history in the gospel narrative. The Old Testament is the New Testament revealed, and the New Testament is in the Old Testament concealed. You cannot go through Grace's door without having Mercy's keys!

At the heart of this doctrine of replacement theology is antisemitism, the oldest form of racism on Earth.

Revival is needed in America but it will never come until preachers repent and return to Hebrew hermeneutics as taught by every writer of our New Testament. Every word of the New Testament can be uncovered in the Old Testament, and true Christian doctrines can be understood only with proper Old Testament instruction. It was Christ's model for warning the Hebrews and it is my model for warning modern Christians that they are being led like sheep to a slaughter. Repent and return to the two-edged sword of the word of God and your Christian testimony will become one where sick people are healed, dead people are raised incorruptible, and poor people receive riches unfathomable.

He was crucified upon a cross of wood, yet he created the hill upon which it stood.

Even so come Lord Jesus Christ.

John Burns 7-28-2021.

The Stumbling Block

The church of modern Pergamos is alive and well. You will know them by their theosophy. They are identified as the seat of Satan on earth. They separate the Old Testament, from the New Testament, and they separate God's children Israel from their inheritance. They cast a stumbling block before the people known as Jews, and they are devoutly antisemitic.

Replacement theology was the Roman answer to Christian persecution. After John the apostle had died of natural causes in Ephesus, Romanized gentile clergy began a gnostic heresy. Augustine, Clement of Rome, and many more Romanized men, began teaching that God had replaced Israel and the Jewish people with Christianity gleaned only from the pages of the New Testament. They began the cult of the Nicolaitans. These men have done the most damage to the modern denominational church experience.

At the heart of this heresy is eugenics. This is an ancient philosophy begun by Greek stoic writers claiming they were the well born stock. All other people are inferior in wisdom, knowledge, and understanding. They sought to control thought as it pertained to all things about God. What is the foundation for this unforgivable heresy?

In Revelation 3 we have Christ, using the model of Baalim to teach us where it began. Numbers 22 introduces the world to the Mesopotamian prophet Baalim. Jesus Christ uses him to establish the fact that socio-political-racist elite men, were separating Jewish believers from their inheritance in Christ. Salvation is of the Jew first and then the Greek. Salvation has never been earned it is imputed. The Jews have the same way back to God as Gentile unbelievers. The cross of Christ.

Baalim was hired for money to curse the fledgling nation of Israel as they wondered in the Midian desert after God delivered them from Egyptian bondage. Baalim has a name that is a duality. He was a Gentile prophet who was asked to curse God's people. He was offered incredible wealth and power if he would cast a curse on God's children. Preachers today, are the modern seat of Satan on earth if their teachings continue what Baalim started in Midian. God has not changed on how he views the nation of Israel.

The name Israel is God's way of saying how he views every person in history. Israel was the name God gave Jacob the deceiver once God had justified him according to faith. Israel translates as one who wrestles with God and wrestles with men. That is my struggle. I wrestle with the thought of both, and I discern how God sees me through the eyes of the entire two-edged sword of the word of God. I cannot understand the grace of God offered on Calvary until I understand the mercy God continually offered Israel in the Old Testament. Mercy will always be the mechanism in our lives by which God will reward you with grace.

Western Greek seminaries are complicit in this heresy. I have applied to 19 of them. When I visit their president of the seminary, I always ask for their organized systemized theology. I ask them if they teach Israelology? I have yet to receive God's answer. Israel makes up 87% of the Bible's content. Why do they not teach a potential minister of God's plan about his people? The answer is simple. Eugenic racism.

Money from government subsidies and tax breaks has kept them in a state of bondage. It was silent denominational pulpits that allowed the Holocaust and the same preachers are silent again. They are scared to stand up for the nation of Israel and the remnant of Jewish believers God has protected here in America. Their days are numbered.

The fear of the Lord is the beginning of wisdom. These men and women fear government more than righteous judgement. They fear losing monetary market share more than they fear God for not leading people away from eugenics. They create doctrines that are not based in Hebrew hermeneutics. Their theories of interpretation are all Western. The Bible is an Eastern book. Not one writer of the Bible was not Jewish. The Old Testament is the New Testament revealed, and the New Testament is in the Old Testament concealed. It is one book. Whoever adds to or takes away from the words of the prophecy of this book, God will add to him the plagues contained there-in.

God knew what Baalim was up to. Baalim left Mesopotamia after being offered money to curse Israel. Modern preachers accept wages for their message. Their Churches follow an American business model that God did not establish. The only person to earn a wage from Jesus Christ's death, burial, and resurrection was Judas! God will get the last laugh.

Baalim was intercepted by an angelic messenger on his way to cursing Israel. His donkey could see the angel, why could he not? He was blinded by greed. A man who once heard from God and prophesied to those living in the Pagan world, was now willing to accept a wage for the message God had given him. Baalim was a tough nut to crack. What was God's response to Baalim's unbelief?

God sent a Jackass to warn Baalim. He is using me as a modern donkey to the pastors, preachers, and teachers as to their ignorance to all things Israel. I believe their antisemitism and ancestor worship keeps them from believing the entire message of God's word. 1 Chronicles 12:32 reminds us that the children of Issachar knew the times and the seasons as it pertained to Israel. Prophecy is pattern and these men will ignore the times to keep their income as pastors and preachers, just like the Pharisees and Sadducees.

We are living in the times the Bible says more about than even the times Jesus Christ walked the earth. Israel is back in the land and prospering. Our current President is antisemitic. He has advanced policies that will condemn America to the abandonment wrath of God. I suspect the American economy will collapse on Elul 29 in the year 2022 just like the Bible says. We have gone the way of Baalim and repentance is required or all your church services will amount to nothing. The seven-year tribulation awaits all those who curse Israel as a nation and all those who deny anyone salvation alone in Yeshua ha Messiah.

Racism and Eugenics are an ancient paradigm. They are present in modern Christian churches and the most dangerous doctrine for anyone claiming faith in Jesus Christ is replacement theology. It makes God a liar and it nullifies every covenant that God says were eternal. Genesis 12 is the nucleus for receiving blessing in this life or the next. He who blesses the children of Abraham will be blessed and he who curses the children of Abraham would be cursed. Forever. God cannot learn and God cannot Lie. He is the God of Abraham, Isaac, Jacob, and Joseph. He is the Lion of the tribe of Judah. He will soon be instructed to go retrieve me, his bride, at the sound of the trumpet. I will fulfill God's will for my life calling Christians out of these heretical churches to help them receive all the precious promises God offered to every person ever born of a woman if they would believe his entire WORD!

That word became flesh and dwelt among us. He is the subject of every scripture ever written. He is Jewish and he desires to redeem all who would believe to the Jew first and then the Greek. Become a Berean Christian and study scripture every day to find out if what I am saying is true. God warned the Hebrews that he does not dwell in houses made with human hands. He Loves you so much he wrote you a book that is your warranty deed over your entire life. The anointing you receive from him is real not counterfeit, you do not need anyone to teach you. Get out of antisemitic heretical churches and get into your bible. Your life will never be the same and your salvation will become one where God's power manifests in the lives of your loved ones.

He was crucified upon a cross of wood, yet he created the hill upon which it stood.

Even so come Lord Jesus Christ.

John Burns 7-25-2021.

Revelation 2:18-29 Unto the Angel of the Church of Thyatira

18 And unto the angel of the church in Thyatira write; These things saith the Son of God, who hath his eyes like unto a flame of fire, and his feet are like fine brass; ¹⁹ I know thy works, and charity, and service, and faith, and thy patience, and thy works; and the last to be more than the first. ²⁰ Notwithstanding I have a few things against thee, because thou sufferest that woman Jezebel, which calleth herself a prophetess, to teach and to seduce my servants to commit fornication, and to eat things sacrificed unto idols. ²¹ And I gave her space to repent of her fornication; and she repented not. ²² Behold, I will cast her into a bed, and them that commit adultery with her into great tribulation, except they repent of their deeds. ²³ And I will kill her children with death; and all the churches shall know that I am he, which searcheth the reins and hearts: and I will give unto every one of you according to your works. ²⁴ But unto you I say, and unto the rest in Thyatira, as many as have not this doctrine, and which have not known the depths of Satan, as they speak; I will put upon you none other burden. ²⁵ But that which ye have already hold fast till I come. ²⁶ And

he that overcometh, and keepeth my works unto the end, to him will I give power over the nations: ²⁷ And he shall rule them with a rod of iron; as the vessels of a potter shall they be broken to shivers: even as I received of my Father. ²⁸ And I will give him the morning star. ²⁹ He that hath an ear, let him hear what the Spirit saith unto the churches.

The Church of Thyatira

This is the fourth church of seven that Jesus Christ dictates a letter to John, and has an angel render into signs. This is the longest of the seven letters, and quite possibly the letter true Christians must understand to be an effective witness in the times we are living in. Thyatira is the picture of the middle age Catholic Church.

Thyatira is the feminine pronoun daughter. It has an ancient history that must be understood to rightly divide the word of truth. To understand Thyatira, one must understand its name in Chaldean, Semiramis.

As the ancient Babylonian history reveals, Semiramis is the consort to Nimrod, the world's first dictator.

He is the descendant of Ham, from Noah. Ham has a name that transliterates as ruddy red and hairy. That was the way Nimrod appeared, and it is the way his descendants look. Nimrod became a warrior and hunter. It is probable his kingdom was under the influence of the fallen angels who had male offspring with the daughters of Adam.

The legend has it that Semiramis was married to one of Nimrod's generals. As king of the entire world, he wanted Semiramis, and apparently, he got her.

She became Nimrod's consort. She eventually had Nimrod killed after she became pregnant probably by a fallen angel. Her sun was called the son of God. His name was Tammuz 1

The Babylonians began to worship Tammuz and he was venerated as the sun god. This legend became the model by which all pagan religions developed their religion's venerating the sun, the moon, and the twelve-star constellations, identified in the book of Job, as the mazzaroth. Astrology has its roots in Babylon with Nimrod and Semiramis.

Nimrod made himself the high priest of the Babylonian religion and assumed the name Pontifex Maximus. He was both the king of Babylon and the high priest of the religion birthed in Babylon where syncretism was first practiced by pagan Nimrod and Semiramis. They mixed worship of the creation, with the worship of all kinds of fertility rights in men and women. It was the Babylonians who introduce the world to Baal and Ashtoreth.

Baal is the god of war and he was venerated as the planet Mars. The reason for this is at the time of Nimrod, earth and mars were on resonant orbits. They would have passed by each other very closely.

Mars would have appeared 70 times bigger than the moon and the planet was visible with the naked eye. Gravity was affected, and tidal waves and other physical phenomenon the Babylonians experienced because of Mars flying so close to earth, caused them to begin worshipping the planets, the stars that surrounded them, and the sun and the moon. The first astronomical structures for viewing the planets were constructed by the pagan Babylonians.

Their entire culture revolved around combining worship of their King and Queen with worshipping the entire created universe. Semiramis constructed groves complete with phallic symbols for the deification of the woman. The entire Babylonian religion venerated reproduction and the worship of the woman. Semiramis is the catalyst by which men and women began to believe in fertility based upon celestial alignment. The first calendars were established in Babylon. 12 months with a constellation venerated for each month of the year based upon the days it took for the sun to be reborn at the winter solstice.

This holiday was celebrated with the worship of the rebirth of the Sun on the shortest solar day of the year. It fell in the 12th month of the Babylonian calendar. It celebrated the birth of Tammuz as the sun God on the winter solstice between the 21st and 25th days of the 12th month of the Babylonian calendar.

When Persia under Cyrus the great conquered Babylon, the high priest and the temple priests and priestesses escaped to western Turkey to the Lydian town of Euhippia. The King of Euhippia took the name Pontifex Maximus and welcomed the escaping priests from Babylon to the now renamed town Semiramis.

The Babylonian religion had now migrated to the center of the Greek world and the Lydians combined it with the worship of Zeus at Pergamos, the temple town of Thyatira was renamed again with a Greek rendering of the Persian name of Semiramis. Thyatira is the town where John started the 1st century Church 13 kilometers from Pergamos.

Christianity had married the Greek world at Pergamos and now it would consolidate temporal power in the town of Thyatira. The high priest adopted the Babylonian title pontifex maximus. The winter solstice was renamed sol Invictus under the Romans, and the Roman priesthood was fully adopted from Babylon at Thyatira. Complete with the 12th month the Romans would adopt as the day the sun was reborn during the celebration of Saturnalia during the winter solstice. The worship of Caesar as pontifex maximus was begun in Thyatira.

Christmas was born and brought into Christian houses for men had not yet begun to build temples for the veneration of pagan fertility holidays named churches. Thyatira is where men claiming to be priests of God began to seek earthly power and titles. The Catholic church of the middle age, can be traced to Thyatira, through Semiramis all the way back to Babylon.

Thyatira is where Romanized Christianity was forced upon the world and the worship of the female deity produced temple priestesses. They served the temple priests in the capacity of temple prostitutes and they set up the groves of Asherah.

Astrology and the worship of angels was begun in Babylon and adopted by the priests and priestesses of Thyatira. Their vestures were black robes with white collars.

In Thyatira the system of organized religion with a hierarchy of priests based upon faithful service to the queen of heaven was begun at Babylon and migrated to western Turkey, and on into the Roman Catholic church. Deacons, priests, bishops, Cardinals all the way through to the Pope who takes the ancient Babylonian title Pontifex Maximus.

The Roman solar calendar was adopted in Thyatira to deal with the Jewish problem. God's calendar found in the Old Testament was replaced with the 12-month Julian calendar in Thyatira. It is the same calendar every western nation adopted and still uses today. God is not on this calendar. It is antisemitic and against the calendar Jesus Christ actually worshipped on during his ministry to the lost sheep of Israel.

Thyatira is the church Jesus Christ reveals himself to as The Son of God. They had begun the queen of heaven paradigm from Babylon, and continued it with the worship and veneration of Mary as bigger than the worship of Jesus Christ. They had begun to worship men in the flesh and the Pope would actually claim infallibility as only the perfect Christ possesses. All have sinned and fall short of the glory of God. The Church of Thyatira is explicitly warned that if they do not become overcomers as outlined by John in the letter of 1 John 5 Vs. 4. Who is he that is an overcomer, but he that Jesus Christ is the Son of God?

Our next edition will identify that woman Jezebel from the Old Testament beginning in 1 Kings 18. She alone has been responsible for more death, hell and the grave than any woman in history. She is the first woman in history to order an inquisition upon the Jewish people in Judea. Her pattern was continued by the Roman Catholic queen Isabella of Spain. The Nazi's became the means by which the Catholic Pope would authorize the murder of Jewish children in Europe to separate them from their earthly rewards and their future heavenly inheritance.

He was crucified upon a cross of wood yet he created the hill upon which it stood.

Even so come Lord Jesus Christ.

The Babylonian Legend

The celebration of the birth of Tammuz, to Semiramis and Nimrod, is still accepted as a Christian holiday in the America I love. Does it qualify as worshipping other gods beside the Trinity?

Ecclesiastes 7:1 reminds a believer they are not to celebrate the day of one's birth but to celebrate the day of one's death.

Would Jesus Christ do something contradictory to the word of God as the sinless Lamb? I think not. To celebrate the birth of Jesus Christ on the winter solstice is a fable. Jesus Christ was born in the Hebrew month of Nisan.

Nisan is the first month on the Hebrew calendar. It occurs in spring. The lambs that were born for the purpose of being sacrificed for the remission of Israel's sins, are only born in spring.

This is confirmed when the shepherds were guarding their flocks by night. The only time shepherds guard their flocks at night is during the birthing season, when the sheep are most vulnerable to predators. Sheep born for the sacrifice of sins are only born in the town of Bethlehem even to this day!

Hebrew Rabbis do not celebrate pagan fertility holidays to include the day of their birth. Jesus Christ our Jewish rabbi was no different. Roman Catholicism gave us the celebration of Christmas, and it is totally pagan.

The Babylonians celebrated the birth of Tammuz as the son of God by going into a forest and cutting down an Erez tree. This is the genus pinacea. A fir or pine tree. This is referenced in Jeremiah 10:4.

Why do you do like the heathens? Why do you cut down and decorate a pine tree? Decorate it with silver and gold, adorn it with the star known as the sun of the morning. This is a reference to the planet Saturn.

The Romans would adopt this celebration in the month of December explicitly to deny Jesus Christ's heritage as the Jewish messiah. Saturnalia is the star and planet assigned to none other than Lucifer himself. The religion it birthed is called Luciferianism. Saturn is the planet or star visible in the morning sky during the winter solstice.

The celebration of the birth of Tammuz as the son of God was adopted by Romanized Christians from Thyatira and Babylon.

Babylon had another feature to this holiday. They would cut and burn a Yule log. The word Yule is the Chaldean word for an infant. The worship of Tammuz was highlighted with the sacrifice of infants upon altars superheated by the burning of logs under brass altars. This was done to recognize Nimrod as the sun god and Semiramis as the queen of heaven.

America does it at the convenient altar of the womb of the mother. Americans celebrate abortion, each time you do like Jeremiah warned us not to do, celebrate this holiday as believers.

All pagan traditions come from the Babylonian legends. Babel was the place from which Nimrod led the first rebellion after the flood. I believe he was under the influence of the giants who escaped Noah's flood. These Nephillim will return after the man of lawlessness is revealed and the Satanic trinity is revealed unto the world during the period know as Daniel's 70th week.

Jesus Christ warned us that such as in the days of Noah, so shall the coming of the son of man be. Angel worship began at Babylon, will continue very soon in Churches across America. I wonder if Christian pastors will recognize the Nephillim courting their daughters in church?

Will you be able to recognize the sons of God from the Old Testament book of Genesis chapter 6?

Revelation 2:18-29 Unto the Angel of the Church of Thyatira

Jesus Christ adjured all 7 churches to exchange each letter. Every church has a little bit of each in all of them. Do you believe Jesus Christ is happy we have stopped believing in the truth of the Bible? Do you believe he is happier with born again Christians celebrating Babylonian traditions, than believing every word of the Bible? I am going to stick with the Bible. As for me and my house we will serve the Lord Jesus Christ!

Nimrod's rebellion had lasting implications in the entire known world at the time. The Babylonian legends he and Semiramis began, migrated into Egypt, Phoenecia, Tyre, Sidon, Greece and beyond to our current standing as the second iteration as the Roman empire outlined in Daniel 2.

Thyatira is the Greek rendering of the Babylonian name for Semiramis. A great temple to her was built by the original trade guilds established in Lydia. Those trade guilds each venerated a pagan god. Nothing has changed. Today we call them trade unions.

The church of Thyatira was told by Christ he knew their works. He told them they were committing fornication. Biblically, fornication is to worship any other gods other than the trinity. At Thyatira the temple priests and priestesses were prostituting themselves to celebrate fertility in women. Apparently, this is a veiled reference to the many fornications Thyatira allowed to migrate into Christian worship. To worship Babylonian gods and celebrate their holiday is fornication to God our trinity.

We are introduced to the Old Testament character Jezebel in the letter to Thyatira. She is the wife of King Ahab from 1 Kings 18. She was the daughter of Eth-Baal the king of Sidon, and priest of Astarte. The Golden egg of Astarte was worshipped.

The idol assigned to Astarte was the body of a naked woman and the head of a bunny rabbit. Another gift from Babylon through ancient Israel is the worship of Ishtar, or Astarte, the Phoenecian fertility deity on what Christians call Easter.

Ahab was king in the northern kingdom of Israel. He ushered in the worst time in the entire Old Testament. The Popes in Rome have ushered in the worst times in the New Testament period.

Jezebel was his queen. She adopted the fertility holidays first begun in Babylon under Semiramis.

Worst of all, Jezebel wiped out the blood line of Naboth to secure his land and tribal inheritance. She did not just kill Naboth, she had every living member of his family killed to steal his vineyard. That vineyard is the Garden of Gethsemane. Where the living vine would pray before being brought to the place of the skull to die for you and me. Hallelujah!

This is the first inquisition in history, and it began the paradigm of the Roman Catholic church murdering the Jews and confiscating their property, throughout the period known as the dark and middle-ages. It was continued by King Ferdinand and Queen Isabella of Spain, which led to the founding of America by Jews and Puritans leaving Europe to escape persecution from within the Roman church. It would carry all the way through to the holocaust of World War II and the final 7 years of gentile history will see the Satanic trinity of Catholic Pope, the man of lawlessness out of the western leg of the Roman empire, unite with an Assyrian dictator to exalt themselves above everything that is called God.

Jezebel continued the pattern begun in Babylon as the so-called queen of heaven. The deification of the woman was continued with Jezebel. She called herself a prophetess just like the Catholic church refers to itself as the mother church and queen from heaven. Queen Isabella referred to herself as a Roman Catholic Queen from heaven.

Jesus Christ's reference to himself as the Son of God directly contradicts queen of heaven worship, and the worship of all pagan Babylonian legends. He is coming back soon. Is Christmas more important than thus says the Lord?

Pagan practices first migrated into Israel all the way into the Christian church experience 1 John 5:4 is the method for understanding overcoming faith.

He was crucified upon a cross of wood yet he created the hill upon which it stood.

Even so come Lord Jesus Christ.

Works Replaced God's Grace

Thyatira is the longest letter Jesus Christ penned to his body and his bride. He reminds Thyatira he can see everything they do, and they are found wanting. Their works of charity had replaced the written revealed word of God. They had become completely antisemitic and they were comfortable in their traditions even though every Roman tradition is pagan and against God's perfect will.

I was raised as a Roman Catholic. I served as an altar boy from the age of seven through the age of twelve. I began to read the Latin Vulgate when I was nine. I opened the book of Daniel to the 10th chapter verse 11. For the first time in my life, the God of creation spoke to me through the Bible, and it scared me tremendously. The Bible contradicted everything I experienced as a young boy and I began to question my ancestors, my teachers, my priests, my parents and everyone in a position of authority over my life. I was completely confused about all things God.

Joining the Army, I found a place where I could spread my wings and travel to the places I was reading about in the Bible. The last act of mercy from a loving God while in uniform was to allow me to visit Rome while stationed in Italy. I found exactly what Martin Luther found, paganism was alive and well and actually prospering in the world through the influence of the Roman Catholic Popes.

The Popes have claimed infallibility claiming to be free from the influence of sin. For all have sinned and fall short of the glory of God. Strike 1.

The leadership of the Popes have led to more deaths of Christians and Jews than any other religion in history. Strike 2.

The hoarding of wealth and the hierarchy of priests, bishops, cardinals, and Popes are exactly what Jesus Christ said he hates, the deeds of the Nicolaitans. Jesus Christ is our one mediator between God and man. We do not need any man to teach us the things of God, that is what makes Christianity real and all other religions false. 1 John 2:27. For the anointing you have received from me is real not counterfeit, for you do not need that any man teach you. Jesus Christ established his church on the Hebrew celebration of Shavuot: we call it Pentecost.

The Holy Spirit was given to 120 Jewish believers in the upper room on the Hebrew feast of first-fruits. The world's first Christians were Jewish. The book of Revelation reveals the last Christians saved will also be the Jewish remnant who cry out hosanna, blessed is he who comes in the name of the Lord, as they look upon him whom they have pierced. This will occur at the end of the tribulation of the last days which Jesus Christ warns Thyatira they will go through if they do not repent and return to the entire written word found in both Testaments of our most Holy Bible. Teshuva!

So, what did Jesus Christ teach us through the Church of Thyatira?

Pagan practices crept into the Roman Church very early on in the ministry of John the Apostle. The marriage of Church and state begun at Pergamos was finalized and continued now for 2000 years in Thyatira.

Roman holidays replaced the sabbaths Jesus Christ established in the Genesis calendar.

Birthdays, Christmas, Easter, Mother's Day, Father's Day, Valentine's Day, funerals. These are all pagan practices. They have nothing to do with the death burial and resurrection of Jesus Christ. Thyatira is warned that it will go through the tribulation, and God will kill her children if they do not repent and return to the written word of God, and stop worshipping on Roman fertility holidays. God is not playing let's make a deal. He gave us his word and warned us not to add to or take away from it or we would suffer the plagues contained within. Covid 19 is God's final warning to those practicing any of these pagan holidays.

The word covid is the Latin word for crown. 19 is the exact number of years God warned Israel after he allowed the first attack on the nation in 605 BC by the Assyrian Nabopollasser. His son Nebuchadnezzar would finish the conquest when he sacked Jerusalem, tore down the walls, destroyed their three-dimensional temple, deported every person to Babylon for 70 years. I believe America's fate will be much worse. This occurred in 586 BC, exactly 19 years after allowing the first attack.

We have allowed for the worship of every pagan deity venerated from Babylon, into western Turkey, into Rome and west to America. Our nation is under the abandonment wrath of God and soon, Jesus Christ will remove his bride as America falls and takes her place as the Iron fully hardened ready to persecute Jews here at home in America. Thyatira and her believers will have one chance during the tribulation to believe in Christ, and it will lead to their martyrdom.

Works replaced grace and also replaced Jesus Christ as messiah in Rome under the Roman Catholic hierarchy. I beg my Catholic friends and relatives to repent and return to God's word found in the Bible.

Thyatira is warned that it will go through the tribulation of the last seven years of gentile government on Earth if they do not repent. This Church is given the chance to repent for 2,000 plus years. Do you hear the still soft voice of God calling you home to salvation alone in Christ's death, burial, and resurrection?

Thyatira led to the reformation of Luther as identified by Christ as the Church of Sardis. I warn those who follow the denominational model the reformation birthed, that Jesus Christ tells Sardis they are dead. Their only hope is resurrection leading to a belief in the entire Bible and move away from antisemitism.

The rapture of the bride of Christ is on our near horizon. It is our blessed hope as true born-again believers in Christ. Thus says the Lord must replace Roman traditions and pagan holidays, or all of your church attendance will have been in vain!

He was crucified upon a Cross of wood yet he created the hill upon which it stood.

Even so come Lord Jesus Christ.

John Burns 9-5-2021.

Revelation 3:1-6 Unto the Angel of the Church of Sardis

3 And unto the angel of the church in Sardis write; These things saith he that hath the seven Spirits of God, and the seven stars; I know thy works, that thou hast a name that thou livest, and art dead. ²Be watchful, and strengthen the things which remain, that are ready to die: for I have not found thy works perfect before God. ³Remember therefore how thou hast received and heard, and hold fast, and repent. If therefore thou shalt not watch, I will come on thee as a thief, and thou shalt not know what hour I will come upon thee. ⁴Thou hast a few names even in Sardis which have not defiled their garments; and they shall walk with me in white: for they are worthy. ⁵He that overcometh, the same shall be clothed in white raiment; and I will not blot out his name out of the book of life, but I will confess his name before my Father, and before his angels. ⁶He that hath an ear, let him hear what the Spirit saith unto the churches.

The Reformation Church of Sardis

As Christians were reeling from the inquisition carried out by the Pope and his inquisitor Thomas de Torquemada, a young law student traveled to Rome. On his way he would encounter an incredible lightning storm that changed his life and his trajectory.

Martin Luther would travel to Rome and be troubled by what he saw as he searched the scriptures daily. Habbakuk 2:4 became his life's scripture. The just shall live by his faith.

Martin Luther would return to Wittenburg and pen his famous 95 theses that identified pagan practices Luther had noted, that were not at all scriptural. This act would officially open what we call the Reformation.

Martin Luther would be excommunicated from the Catholic church. He would be supported by the German princes who felt like the Pope had way too much power as nationalism began to take hold in Europe. Luther was not however, responsible for the reformation, he was only a catalyst.

The Waldenses, the Huguenots and many other break-away groups had been persecuted and killed by the Popes in Rome years before Luther penned the 95 theses. Arguably the reformation was begun by common people who began to have access to the Bible as the printing press and movable type birthed the first translations of the Latin Vulgate into German. This Bible, the Guttenberg version was being distributed throughout France, England, Italy and Germany. Man, once again had access to the scriptures without the need for any man to teach them. The reformation was born in the houses of true believers.

Men began to realize faith was not a corporate event. Families began to reject the three-dimensional church model advanced by Catholicism as they strove to unite Church and state with the Pope being the supreme power over European Monarch's. The reformation returned the Church temporarily to its Acts of the Apostles roots. Men began to hold Bible study in their homes of their friends. No need for any priest, or church hierarchy to teach them the things of God. It would not last.

Luther had realized faith was between he and God. However, he continued to separate the Old Testament from the New Testament and he advanced the replacement theology narrative. He became more and more antisemitic toward all things Jewish. While acknowledging that we are justified by Jesus Christ's death upon the cross, he denied Christ's inheritance promised by God to Mary when Jesus Christ was in her womb. He did not understand that every letter in the Old Testament was pointing us toward Christ in Prophecy.

87% of the content of the Bible was written to Jewish people descended from Abraham through faith in God's entire plan of redemption. National Israel and spiritual Israel have different futures. To not understand both, is what is wrong with the denominational Church birthed during the reformation. They all began to do what was right in their own eyes. Doctrines of educated men replaced thus says the Lord.

Sardis is the city in western Turkey settled by the Lydians in 1500 BC. It was an incredibly wealthy city. It was at the crossroads of the world's most important trade routes. People prospered monetarily in Sardis in antiquity. Gold and silver coins were first minted in Sardis by the Lydians.

Sardis boasted of its library, gymnasium and synagogue in the city center. Residents of Sardis had pagan temples to the fertility cults that migrated from Babylon when conquered by Cyrus the great. Church and state were inseparable. The reformation of Luther did not fix man's desire to be married to the world. Jesus Christ warned Sardis that they are a dead Church. Sardis had nothing good said about it by Messiah. I pray you will hear him now!

Sardis is a precious stone. It is red in color. The Sardis stone was the last stone in the high priest's ephod. It was also identified as one of the covering stones created in Lucifer. The Sardis stone was identified as the stone which represented the tribe of Benjamin. His name is transliterated into English as son of the right hand.

Jesus Christ identifies himself in the letter to Sardis as he who has the seven spirits of God, and he holds the seven stars, which are the angels of the seven churches. These are titles reserved for God found in the Old Testament. Jesus Christ was alerting Sardis to the fact that he is the third person of the creative name of God found in Genesis 1. He was stating the fact that he was the God who entered our world that he created in the womb of a virgin Jewish girl. God became the seed of the woman as he promised in Genesis 3. God's seed was Jesus Christ. Jesus Christ is God!

Jesus Christ warns Sardis to return to the testimony that Jesus Christ died to pay your sin debt. He was raised from the dead to raise us all from dead religious practices to include denominational thinking.

Jesus Christ is building a kingdom based on inclusion not tribalism. He does not save us to give us the right to judge anybody but ourself. The entire Bible was written to every person born of a woman for them to understand what their creator did for them.

The church looks like the world it was called out of when they believe it is their job to police morality in the fallen world. The Church will never get anyone saved if they believe it is their job to shame people into believing in what Jesus Christ did for all of us on the cross. I have never shamed anyone into being my friend, and neither did the Jesus Christ you claim to believe in. Repent and return to belief in the entire two-edged sword of the Word of God.

Old Testament study is required if you are ever going to understand the Christ who is redeeming his entire creation. Teshuva! Repent and return to belief in Christ as creator.

He was crucified upon a cross of wood, yet he created the hill upon which it stood.

Even so come Lord Jesus Christ.

John Burns 9-9-2021.

Thou Hast a Name

The church of Sardis is the first of two churches about which Jesus Christ has nothing good to say. This church replaced the message of the blood of Jesus Christ cleansing a sinner from all unrighteousness, with doctrines found in the Torah and ended in the Gospels, to include the need for external water baptism.

By believing God replaced Israel with the gentile New Testament denominations is exactly why Jesus Christ calls Sardis the dead church. The Old Testament is the story of our pre-destination, our calling, our justification, and our eventual glorification, as told in the lives of God's people.

We are introduced to God's eternal mercy in the Old Testament. Mercy is the only key that opens the door of grace found in the life of Messiah. Mercy is required every day in our Christian walk. If the church would get back to asking for mercy, grace will appear and the Holy Spirit will use men of God to bring miracles back into Christian faith.

God has never changed! Men change constantly like the weather. The persecution from the Jews in Jerusalem in the Ephesian and Smyrna Church ages led to the marriage of church and state at Pergamos and total compromise with Pagan Rome was consummated permanently in the city and church of Thyatira. But the reformation church is the one Christ calls the dead church.

What is the cure outlined by Christ in this letter? 1 John 5:4 is where we learn to become an overcomer in Christ. But Jesus Christ admonishes Sardis to repent and return to his two-edged sword, and believe every word of the Bible as literal and being fulfilled.

Study to show yourself approved only after losing all denominational doctrines, and pre-suppositions taught first by your ancestors. 1 John 2:27 for the anointing you have received from me is real not counterfeit, you do not need that any man to teach you. Become a Berean Christian and study the scripture daily to find out if what John Burns is saying were true.

Jesus Christ admonishes that after they repent, they should return to his doctrine of imminence taught as the rapture of the bride of Christ from within the body of Christ. This is the most important doctrine not understood or being taught from scripture. Jesus Christ's reward for his crucifixion was to receive a virgin bride taken from all the nations of the earth during the gentile church age. After the dowry for our marriage to Christ was paid on Calvary, we were commanded to eagerly await the return of Messiah to claim his bride at the sound of the trumpet in the clouds.

The Church of Sardis has no hope. Of these three abideth faith, hope, and love. You cannot get to the blessed hope of the rapture without first experiencing the faith of Jesus Christ found in the Bible narrative.

The Old Testament is where we learn of God's intention to become the Lamb slain on Calvary. Faith in who it was on the cross and why he had to die is at the core of Christ faith. He had to die to redeem man to God and remove the curse on the entire creation due to Lucifer's rebellion. Jesus Christ's hope is that one day God will sound the trumpet and tell the Son to go retrieve your bride I promised you prior to creating this world inhabitable for humans. We are supposed to be the virgin bride of Christ, yet we deny his covenant relationship with our Jewish ancestors by teaching replacement theology.

The red stone of Sardis is representative of the reformation churches and denominations it spurned. It is the precious stone assigned to the tribe of Benjamin and the last stone of the high priest's ephod. I believe a Benjamite will be the head of national Israel before the return of Messiah to the earth at the end of the last seven years of Gentile reign on earth. These seven years are preceded by the rapture.

The purpose for the rapture cannot be understood from the New Testament alone. The Book of Daniel is where we learn of the 70th week of desolation upon the stiff-necked Jewish remnant in the holy land after the rapture. The week is identified as the times of Jacob's trouble. It is reserved for the final chastening of the Jewish people and the nations of the earth who have denied God's entire plan of redemption. The bride of Christ will be removed before this period begins. Are you the virgin bride of Christ? Are you eagerly awaiting the return of your risen bridegroom? Repent, for the kingdom of God is near!

Jesus Christ's desire for Sardis is for them to get under the blood of the Lamb, return to understanding God's plans for your life by becoming a student of scripture. Find your own life in the lives of our Old Testament Jewish ancestors. Pray continually for the return of Messiah to retrieve you as his bride. Ask for mercy every day, and never be afraid to share the reasons for the joy that is within you.

Joy has a name. It is Yeshua ha messiah in Jesus Christ's native tongue. We English speakers refer to him as Jesus the

Christ. He died to pay the only debt that matters when we die; our sin debt to God as creator.

The Old Testament is Jesus Christ in prophecy. The Gospels are Jesus Christ in history. The Acts of the Apostles was Jesus Christ in the Church. The Pauline epistles are Jesus Christ in practical Christian application. The Revelation is Jesus Christ in Glory.

To understand Revelation, one must travel to every book of the Bible to unlock the signs Jesus Christ commanded the angel to render what John saw into those Old Testament signs. The Revelation is the only book that promises a blessing for reading it as a believer.

Hebrews reminds us that Jesus Christ is the topic of every scripture found in the Bible. Of the abundance of the letter, it is written of me. Please begin a new relationship with the Jesus Christ of the Old Testament and New Testament. Jesus will appear in your life as a blessing to everyone you come in contact with.

He was crucified upon a cross of wood yet he created the hill upon which it stood.

Even so come Lord Jesus Christ.

John Burns 9-27-2021.

I Go to Prepare You a Place

John 14. Jesus Christ comforting the apostles as to his and their future. What is the teaching mechanism God has used to prove he is a God who keeps his covenants from generation to generation?

The Church of Sardis is admonished for not eagerly awaiting the return of Messiah to receive us to him. The people called out of the world around them, now look exactly like the world they claim to be not part of. Christ reminded us we are in the world but not of the world.

In my father's house are many mansions, if it were not so I would have told you. I go to prepare you a place.

The reason Sardis is told they are not eagerly awaiting Christ's return to receive them unto himself, is because they deny the Levirite marriage covenant found in Genesis 22 between God and Abraham and his descendants forever. Once Abraham believed God, it was accounted unto him for righteousness. The same way Christians are saved today.

Faith in what God has given us in his word, he is faithful and just to be the author and finisher of our faith. He activates your faith. He enhances your faith through study of his entire two-edged sword. He will finish your faith as he has promised Gentiles when the mystery was revealed to Paul, that Gentiles would be fellow heirs with God's people Israel.

Because Isaac was willing to be sacrificed for what Abraham taught him about the promise he received from God, that his offspring would sit on the throne of Israel judging all the nations of the earth, Isaac laid his life upon the altar as his father prepared to sacrifice him, knowing God would raise his son from the dead. Sound Familiar?

Jesus Christ received the same blessing Isaac received, a gentile bride from the ancestors of Abram the Chaldean. Genesis 24 is the pattern established by God to find Jesus Christ a gentile bride from the pagan nations of the earth. God is searching for those rare believers willing to become the virgin bride of Christ. To do that, Holy Spirit anointing is required. Your ability must be replaced by Christ's humility!

Abraham instructs Eleazar to go back to the land of his nativity and find Isaac a virgin bride from amongst his ancestors. These were polytheist family members, and Abraham wanted his son to marry one of their daughters. Eleazar transliterates in English as Comforter. The same comforter God sends to unbelievers now to find his son a bride. The pattern established in Genesis 23.

A virgin in the Bible written by God, is one who does not defile themselves with the gods of the pagan government around them. She would never worship any other God than the one established in Genesis 1. She would never follow any other worship calendar than the one Jesus Christ worships on, for the Genesis calendar points to everything Jesus! Hallelujah!

When the father sends the comforter to find Christ a bride, the dowry has already been paid. After Isaac laid willingly on Abraham's altar, God supplied a Lamb. He supplied a lamb for your hand in marriage. Are you acting like the virgin bride of Christ? Your dowry was paid on Calvary. Eleazar brought Rebekah's family ten camels laden with the treasures of Abraham's house, to prove they would supply all of her needs, forever. Hallelujah!

Upon dying upon the cross, Christ was to receive a virgin bride. When Rebekah's family accepted the offer, she would have been veiled. Isaac would be preparing her a room addition on Abraham's home.

Jesus Christ returned to his father's house to build you and I a mansion. Hallelujah! We are behind the veil, eagerly awaiting the return of Messiah to receive us unto himself. A living bridegroom receiving a living bride.

The purpose of the rapture. To remove the bride, before God judges all of the nations of the earth. Ask yourself a question. Would God spend 2,000 years finding his son a bride, only to beat her up for 7 years?

The tribulation is reserved for God to judge his creation, before establishing Christ's throne on earth. The times of Jacob's troubles. Daniel's 70th week. Study to show yourself approved, a workman rightly dividing the word of truth!

This is the most important teaching God has ever revealed to me. When I realized God hates divorce, I realized I was indeed married to Christ and he would never leave me nor forsake me. He is married to me forever, if I accept his eternal mercy, and un-expendable grace, I remain a virgin unwilling to serve the God's of this world, the rapture is my future and I am eagerly awaiting the return of Messiah to receive me unto himself, to be forever with the Lord! Hallelujah!

Christian testimony must become one where Jesus Christ is indeed your only bridegroom. He must become Lord if you intend to rule and reign with him. Crowns will be handed out at the marriage supper of the Lamb which lasts seven years in heaven. It occurs before Christ's returning to the physical earth to establish the millennial kingdom. This kingdom will see the bridegroom ruling with the bride as Christ fulfills the oldest prophecy uttered by Enoch in Genesis: I saw the Lord coming with 10,000 of his saints to rule over all nations of the earth, Hallelujah!

So much is missing from the modern Christian Church experience. This teaching you cannot afford to not understand, for it is the true Christian future. Sardis is warned that they must return to waiting on the Lord from heaven. Sardis is the reformation Church and the denominations it has spawned who deny Christ marriage to his gentile bride. They are not eagerly awaiting return of messiah for they have never learned this teaching established by God in Genesis.

Teshuva! Repent and return unto the entire Bible. It is a sword with two edges. Mercy is the story of our Old Testament ancestors, the stiff-necked Jewish people. Grace is the revelation of Christ redeeming Gentiles also. Both are required to rightly understand the true Christian future.

Have you become so heavenly-minded; you are no earthly good to God?

He loved you so much he desires you to become the virgin bride he intends to present to his Son. Without blemish. Ready to rule and reign for 1,000 years on the earth after the marriage is consummated in heaven. What an amazing story woven into our Bible to teach us just how much God loves his creation! Hallelujah!

He was crucified upon a cross of wood, yet he created the hill upon which it stood.

Even so come Lord Jesus Christ!

John Burns 9-12-2021.

I Will Come on Thee as a Thief

Jesus Christ warns Sardis that they are the church not celebrating that Jesus Christ could return with no prerequisite conditions other than Jesus Christ left at his ascension.

Imminence is how Jesus Christ requires our waiting period of 2,000 years to be experienced. Imminently watching and awaiting the return of our bridegroom from heaven to establish his kingdom.

What is missing from the church message in America today? Is anyone eagerly awaiting the return of Messiah? What awaits those who do not defile themselves with the gods of this world?

Psalm 51 is God's answer to what is needed in church today.

Have mercy upon me oh God according to your lovingkindness, according to the multitude of thy tender mercies blot out my transgressions. Wash me thoroughly from mine iniquity and cleanse me from my sin. For I acknowledge my transgressions and my sin is ever before me. Before thee and thee alone have I sinned and done this evil in your sight that thou may be justified when thou speakest and be clear when thou judgest. Behold I was shapen in iniquity and in sin did my mother conceive me. Behold, thou desire truth in the inward parts, and in the hidden parts thou shalt make me to know wisdom. Purge me with hyssop and I shall be clean, wash me and I shall be whiter than snow. Make me to hear joy and gladness; that the bones thou hast broken may rejoice. Hide thy face from my sins; and blot out all my iniquities. Create in me a clean heart oh God, and renew in me a steadfast spirit. Cast me not away from thy presence and remove not thy holy spirit from me. Restore unto me the joy of thy salvation; and uphold me with thy free spirit. THEN WILL I TEACH SINNERS THY WAYS; AND SINNERS SHALL BE CONVERTED UNTO THEE! Mercy always precedes grace in God's economy.

Sardis is a red stone. Red is the color of the blood which covers our iniquities. The Sardis stone was hard and red. It was polished to a beautiful sheen. God desires to turn us from Sardis to a precious diamond. That requires the humility to ask for forgiveness in not understanding the doctrine of imminence.

Diamonds are many faceted. It takes a long time for diamonds to be precious stones. They are heated, beaten, cut, polished, and loved. Have you allowed God to heat you through unbelief and repented? Are you holding on to religious pre-suppositions practiced by your ancestors? Do you love your Roman traditions more than you love Christ's message? Is looking like the world more important than your Christian conviction? Sin is not your problem. How you intend to answer God for your sin is your problem!

All the church attendance in the world will never pay your sin debt. Following traditions God abhors will end up in your separation from Christ as his bride. Doctrines will never replace <u>relationship to Christ as Bridegroom</u>. Grace is being prostituted in church and God is not happy.

Teshuva! Repent and return unto God in His Word.

God promises those who have not defiled themselves with the gods of this world, that they shall be clothed in white. God promises to not blot His name out of the book of life. He states there are few in Sardis who have not defiled their garments. Are you defiled? Have you served the gods of your ancestors? Is Easter, Christmas, your birthday, Valentine's Day, Memorial Day, or any day government gives you off from work, more important than your betrothal as the bride of Christ, eagerly awaiting his return to claim you as his bride? He is coming back very soon at the sound of the trumpet to retrieve his virgin bride.

Please hear the still soft voice and return to belief in his Bible if you ever had it.

If not, please consider opening your Bible today, asking God for mercy. Ask Him to cover you in the blood of Calvary. And study the scripture daily to see if what John Burns is saying were true. I Love you as Christ loved his Church, and laid down his life for you as his bride. Please become a virgin bride and forgo the gods of this world. Your eternal future depends on it.

Jesus Christ died for very specific reasons with very specific rewards. His reward is to receive us as a virgin bride. His inheritance is to rule over all the nations of the earth for 1,000 years.

The betrothal is happening each time the Holy Spirit visits the heart of an unbeliever to call them home to Christ. Jesus Christ did not die to make bad men good, he died to raise dead men to life.

The most preposterous debt payment plan in human history revolves around God finding his son a bride, and then celebrating his Son's marriage in heaven, before returning with his bride to earth to rule over all the nations who come out of the great tribulation of the last 3 ½ years of gentile reign.

We have been asked by Jesus Christ and Paul to eagerly await his return to retrieve us unto himself. We have been warned by Christ that those who are not waiting are not his bride. The rapture will not find you in heaven celebrating Christ's marriage to his bride.

You have one chance after the rapture to come home to Christ, and heaven as an eternal reward. Martyrdom during the last seven years of gentile rule, when the satanic trinity manifests and unites to stop God from establishing Christ's kingdom in Jerusalem.

John in revelation 4 reminds us that the redeemed are clothed in white, standing around the throne of Messiah, worshipping him in heaven, while the body of Christ is left behind to suffer at the hands of this fallen world.

Please accept Christ's offer of marriage. Know that he is building you a mansion. He will return for you. Your future is secure. Eagerly await his return. Never miss an opportunity to share the reason for the joy that is within you. That joy is your blessed hope and reward for eagerly awaiting Christ's return in the clouds.

He was crucified upon a cross of wood, yet he created the hill upon which it stood.

Even so come Lord Jesus Christ.

9-12-2021 John Burns RLTW.

The Bride Veiled

The first covenant in the Bible established by God is the marriage covenant between one man and one woman. Why was establishing marriage as a biblical paradigm so important to God as creator?

God exists in at least ten special dimensions. His home we call heaven. Who occupies heaven with God?

According to the Bible Elohim created four things. He created the heavens and the earth. He created angels. He created man in His image. Did God create women?

According to the Bible God created man and placed him in a garden. God gave Adam the command to name all of the animals. While naming all of the animals, procreation began in animal species first. Adam posed a question for God: where is my suitable helpmeet?

Adam recognized God had uniquely created the animals with the ability to procreate and only between male and female of the same species. Animals are never homosexual. Their purpose for existence is to provide sustenance for man. Procreation in animals was established as an entropy reduction in creation for man to have continual sustenance. Animals do not engage in sexual intercourse for pleasure alone, it is designed purposely for reproduction.

God's answer to Adam was to put him to sleep and remove a piece of his heart from which he formed the woman as Adam's suitable helpmeet in pro-creation. The man was created to be the Glory of God and woman was brought forth to be the glory of man.

God has two divine attributes. Mercy is an attribute men can learn only after believing in God's single plan of redemption. Mercy is to not receive what we deserve for the wages of sin is death. Sin was atoned for once and for all on the cross of calvary. To believe we need mercy from God is the foundation for Christian witness.

Mercy is the key that opens grace's door. Grace is to receive what we do not deserve and it is totally free. It cannot be earned by outward piety or acts of kindness. Grace is imputed to a sinner when they have the humility to ask for God's mercy. God's mercy is eternal for we exist in the presence of sin.

The need for mercy does not decrease over time. Mercy is needed every hour of every day in our Christian walk. Mercy is the divine attribute God desires Christians learn and apply to the life of every person they encounter. It is mercy alone that will lead a sinner to the cross of Christ, and the grace of Jesus Christ.

Mercy is what Jesus Christ taught the Jews of Jerusalem they needed over their lives. Grace had appeared in Israel and he was telling the children of God they required mercy. Hallelujah. Mercy is what is most needed in the lives of church folk as I pen these words.

The Old Testament is the teaching tool employed by our creator to show us practical reasons why all humans require mercy over their lives. The Jewish people of the Old Testament had been awarded the responsibility of bringing the plan of redemption to a fallen world and they turned it into a religious experience. God does not enjoy religion.

The nation God birthed in Egypt wanted to return to worshipping like their neighbors. They requested God give them a temple. God gave them very specific instructions for worshipping Him in an earthly structure because He knew they would eventually get bored and exchange worship of the creator with worship of the temple God gave them as an appeasement. He had warned them that there was not a temple big enough to contain Him. He had told them He does not dwell in houses made with human hands. I am the Lord and I change not. Jesus Christ never preached in a Church. In fact, none of the writers of the New Testament taught anyone in a church.

The tabernacle Christ desires to inhabit is the three-part tabernacle known as the human condition. The spirit, the soul, and the body of every person born of a woman. The human condition as a pattern for worship was established in the garden when God made Eve from the heart of Adam for the purpose of raising Godly offspring.

There are no female angels. Women hold an exalted position in God's economy. Only Eve was brought forth for the purpose of giving God the seed he required. Jesus Christ would be born of a virgin woman. I can think of no greater reward women can seek than to know they were brought forth to make God's plan complete.

Marriage is the pattern God uses to establish the reward he intended to give Christ for going to the cross. A virgin bride is who God has been seeking through the Holy Spirit for 2,000 years now. Virginity in God's eyes has everything to do with the compromises made in worshipping the gods of this world.

Christmas venerates Saturn as the son of the morning. This is a title reserved for Lucifer who began the cult of worshipping fallen angels in Babylon. Worshippers were required to bring their infants to Babel and throw them on superheated bronze altars.

The word Yule in the Chaldean tongue is the English word infant. The mistletoe is a fertility drug used in Babylon to bring on a woman's reproductive cycle. Hebrews, to include Jesus Christ never worshipped their own birthdays. If Jesus

Revelation 3:1-6 Unto the Angel of the Church of Sardis

Christ did, he would have celebrated his in the month of Nisan in spring.

Easter is the celebration venerating the bunny rabbit fertility deity Ashtarte. The golden egg of Ashtarte is an allusion to the seed of the woman. In biology women have no seed, it is provided by the man in reproduction.

In Babylon, the high priest under the influence of fallen angels, who knew the plans of God to redeem man through the womb of a woman, polluted the story of God's plan to redeem creation through a pure Jewish offspring. Nimrod and Semiramis gave us Tammuz the son born on the winter solstice through an adulterous affair with a fallen angel. All false religions began in Babylon.

The virgin bride of Christ is identified in Revelation as the Churches of Smyrna and Philadelphia alone. The body of Christ is identified as those who pollute themselves with the gods of this world. The other five churches in Revelation who do not repent and stop worshipping these false deities. They will go through the tribulation and have a final chance at eternal life by being martyred during the great tribulation.

The body of Christ will not rule and reign with Christ in his coming kingdom. The bride will receive her crowns in heaven, and return with Messiah to rule and reign with him for 1,000 years. The bride is eagerly awaiting the return of Messiah to receive his hand in marriage as I pen these words.

Many people who sit in church every Sunday singing Lord, Lord will not be raptured. Jesus Christ will reply depart from me worker of iniquity for I knew you not. Church attendance in God's economy is akin to covering your own nakedness with fig leaves and judging others for not doing the same. Blasphemy!

As a virgin bride, my dowry was paid on calvary. Jesus Christ's death paid for everything I need to faithfully await the return of my bridegroom.

He has returned to the house of his father to build me a mansion. Because he has gone, he promised to return and receive me unto himself in the clouds.

The blessed hope of true Christians, the rapture of the bride before the last 7 years of gentile reign on earth. Hallelujah.

Are you the virgin bride of Christ as outlined in the two-edged sword of our Bible?

Is your blessed hope in his imminent return?

As a Christian, my rewards and inheritance were purchased by Christ on Calvary.

My reward is eternal life in heaven.

My inheritance is to rule and reign with Christ over all of the nations of the earth from Jerusalem as the virgin bride of Christ.

My crowns are secure because I believe, and my belief causes me to never be afraid to share the reason for all the joy that is within me.

Joy has a name and a future with me. It is Yeshua ha Messiah or Jesus the Christ. For the Joy that was set before him he endured the cross.

He was crucified upon a cross of wood yet he created the hill upon which it stood.

Even so come lord Jesus Christ.

Joy Through Suffering

The letter to the Church of Sardis is the saddest indictment by a bridegroom to the virgin bride he was promised by God in the womb of Mary. The worst of attributes handed down by their ancestors had taken hold.

At Ephesus they had lost their first love. The apostolic Church begun on the sea of Galilee, migrated into western Turkey. They had become so good at building churches, they forgot to spend time alone with Messiah. Fellowship to Messiah had morphed into corporate gatherings in three dimensional temples where paganism had a foothold.

At Smyrna, God's answer was to allow persecution at the hands of ten specific Roman emperors. From Nero to Diocletian, a lot of Christians were martyred for their testimony that the blood of the Lamb of God had cleansed them from all unrighteousness and his resurrection guaranteed their eternal life.

In Pergamos the underground Christian Church of Smyrna, which had endured about three hundred years of persecution unto death, married the world under Emperor Constantine who Romanized Christianity to the detriment of us all.

Roman holidays were replacing sound Old Testament sabbath worship and Jewish holiday schedule. All for the purpose of joining the pagan fertility cults permeating Roman lives, with a little bit of Jesus Christ.

At Thyatira, The Nicolaitans held complete power. The Babylonian religion had set up permanent residence in Rome. At the head of the Church the ancient Babylonian high priest, Pontifex Maximus. He consolidated power and gave Christianity a Latin touch. An elite priest class of Gnostics now held sway over who God saved. The Jewish origins of Christianity had to be wiped out. Antisemitism became their calling card as the self-proclaimed Queen of Heaven.

Insurrection became the calling card of the Pope in Rome culminating in the holocaust of World War II by a devoutly antisemitic group of Nazi thugs under the banner of the Pope in Rome, and the Lutherans who dominated the country of Germany when Hitler seized power. Ahab and Jezebel are alive in Thyatira and they are still influencing events around the world as I pen these words.

The Pope in Rome is the second person of the Satanic trinity revealed in scripture that will one day unite the house of the sun god with the house of the moon god and the man of lawlessness out of the western leg of the Roman empire. I believe we have watched that event manifest over the last year.

Revelation 3:1-6 Unto the Angel of the Church of Sardis

The worst thing that the middle age church did to believers was hold sway over the word of God. Bibles were not in every house. The priests determined what the people needed to know. The Holy Spirit became a thing of the past. Silent pulpits allowed the inquisition and the Holocaust.

Sardis is the reformation church that began to challenge the authority of Rome. With the aid of the printing press in Germany, the Bible once again became available to the poor man. This event contributed to the beginning of Martin Luther's reformation.

While traveling to Rome to seek a degree in law, a lightning storm scared him into his career in theology. His greatest revelation became the calling of his life, and permeates our Christian testimony today. Habbakuk 2:4 The just shall live by his faith.

Luther did not move away from the three-dimensional building model for meeting in church. He kept the Roman holidays and allowed pagan practices to continue in Lutheran worship to include transubstantiation.

Martin Luther was devoutly antisemitic and he believed the gentile church had somehow replaced the nation of Israel as God's children, not understanding we are grafted into the living vine of Israel through Jesus Christ's resurrection. God will one day save the Jews in Israel as they look upon him whom they have pierced and cry Hosanna, blessed is he who comes in the name of the Lord.

The reformation gave birth to the nation we call home. The city of its founding holds the key to the church of Philadelphia. This is where the agape love of Christ returned the church to its missionary footing. America had become the means by which God intended to take the Gospel and missionary outreach to the entire globe.

Philadelphia is the pearl of great price. The pearl begins as an irritation and becomes desired through time. Time spent with Christ became the Philadelphia calling as she took the Gospel around the globe.

America became the beacon of hope around the globe as she planted the cross of Christ in places most people did nor exist. Has missionary outreach left America and been replaced by Capitalism in church and beyond?

The Philadelphia church is promised it will not go through the tribulation coming upon the entire world. With the persecuted church of Smyrna, Philadelphia will be raptured as the virgin bride of Christ.

Philadelphia was only possible because America became the envy of the world. World War II was a righteous war to save the Jewish remnant in Europe that would contribute to the prophetic founding of the state of Israel. America became wealthy because America's God was taken around the world.

American wealth contributed to worldwide evangelism. With that wealth came the trappings of this world. The church and state were married through tax breaks and elections. The church began to look just like the world they were called out of.

Laodicea would see the American church forgo persecution and missionary outreach in exchange for incredible wealth being horded by men that are wolves in sheep clothing. They have their reward and it is earthly. No one has time for relationship to Christ, there is no joy through suffering, this church needs not the blood of the Lamb purchasing mercy over their lives. Grace is prostituted in Roman religious practices. Nothing good said about Laodicea.

Our answer is Christ's testimony. For the joy that was set before him he endured the cross. Dumb like a lamb, he opened not his mouth. Joy found only in the dimension of human suffering. Washing the feet of society's undesirables. Apathy must be replaced with the world once again saying I need Jesus Christ to cover my sins. Christian witness must be based upon mercy and grace replacing outward piety in dealing with sinners whom God loves, and desires in his kingdom.

Christ ministry involved restoring a prostitute who became the first full gospel evangelist. Christ entrusted her with "I am alive forevermore!"

He restored a leper to the status of whole.

He employed a tax collector, fishermen, a doctor, a traitor, tentmaker, his brothers and even a Roman legionnaire.

He was a carpenter, a shepherd, a rabbi, a prophet, a suffering servant, and coming King.

He died so we might live!

He was crucified upon a cross of wood, yet he created the hill upon which it stood.

Even so come Lord Jesus Christ.

John Burns 10-7-2021.

A Hereditary Priesthood

1 Peter 2:9 Who is Peter speaking too?

Christians in America have no idea what to do with their salvation. They are comfortable gathering in three-dimensional spaces holding the gospel of our Messiah.

They kidnap God for two hours a week on Sunday and maybe Wednesday, and there is absolutely no power in their message or ministry.

The communities they claim to serve are crying out for the kingdom. What will we all do?

The Old Testament is where we are introduced to the priests and kings of ancient Israel. Their lives were chronicled for our edification.

Revelation 1:6 reveals the purpose for our salvation, to become kings and priests of God. Not just preachers, but every person born of a woman who receives justification from God. If you claim salvation in the blood of the Lamb, are you preparing to rule and reign with Christ as kings and priests?

Revelation 3:1-6 Unto the Angel of the Church of Sardis

Do you never open the Bible? Are you comfortable with pagan church traditions?

While men of the reformation consolidated power in denominational churches, replacement theology began to be taught in the first century. The church of Sardis began to teach that the New Testament had somehow replaced the Old Testament. They were teaching that gentile pagan believers, replaced God's people Israel. This heresy makes the God we serve a liar and it makes 87% of scripture irrelevant.

The Jews in Israel have a destiny outlined in our Bible that centers around the 70th week of Daniel. It is the entire subject matter of Revelation from Chapter 4-21. The Jews are the living vine gentile Christians are grafted into. For the church that was given Christ's Grace, they have forgotten that mercy is the only pre-requisite condition for receiving the grace of Messiah.

Mercy is the story of our Old Testament ancestors. They were given the law to teach us all what exactly we need mercy from. They were separated into the priests of Levi and the kings of Judah. It is a lesson in mercy and grace. Kings need mercy to understand responsibility in ruling. Priests require grace in leading people under the cloak of mercy. Mercy is to not receive what we all deserve, for the wages of sin is death.

Mercy is the divine attribute God has been showing our Jewish brethren for a long time. Since the garden of Eden. Mercy is why Abraham met Melchisedec after freeing Lot. He is the King of Salem and prince of righteousness. He had no beginning and no end. He received a tithe of Abraham from the spoils of the enemies of God. He is whom we get our hereditary inheritance and our rewards.

The book of Hebrews in our New Testament is the book that deals with all things priestly. You need the Old Testament wisdom to glean Holy Spirit instruction as to the purposes of God on earth and in your future. As a priest we need instruction to offer the sacrifices of righteousness. The Bereans are our example.

For the Bereans were more noble than those in Thessalonika in that they searched the scriptures daily to find out if what Paul were saying were true. To be a priest in the Kingdom of messiah, knowledge of the Old Testament priests to understand the right and wrong way of offering sacrifices God actually accepts. For I require mercy and not sacrifice says the Lord.

The High priest of our covenant went behind the veil once, for all the sins of the world. The sacrifice he offered as the lamb was none other than Jesus Christ the second person of the creation Godhead. God paid an incredible price for you to serve Him at the altar of sacrifice. Would you rather reign in heaven or rule on earth?

Our priesthood revolves around belief in the death, burial, and resurrection of Messiah. Jesus Christ united the priesthood of Melchisedec with the king of Israel descended from David at his water baptism. He changed water to blood at the last supper. No need to get under the water of baptism if you never intend to serve at the altar of blood given us by Yeshua when he became our high priest.

No one would put new wine into old wineskins. The Jews had required a Mikveh purification ritual each time the high priest was to enter the Holy of Holies behind the veil. Jesus Christ finished the paradigm when he and John transferred the priesthood back upon messiah. Christians become Jews in name only when they require gentiles to get under the water of baptism.

Paul tells us there is one baptism and it is heavenly not earthly. It is the blood baptism achieved on Calvary once and for all on a wooden cross. Only a belief in the blood of the Lamb cleansing you from all unrighteousness required for entrance into Messiah's kingdom.

What is missing in Christian worship is the desire to be resurrected from dead religious thinking steeped in antisemitism. Our high priest is a Jewish rabbi who will one day receive the crown of King David as he returns with his bride to destroy the enemies of God and establish the monarchy promised Judah, David and Mary.

As a King forever God makes it easy. Study the life of king David and figure out why God says in Acts 15 he searched for a man after mine own heart and I found David. David had an attribute God loved. It was his desire to always ask God for mercy when he sinned. It is David who said I do not care what men think I care what God alone thinks. This should be your Christian testimony if you intend to serve in the coming kingdom of our God.

He needs you to activate your royal priesthood inherited at the resurrection of Messiah. Study to show yourself approved, a workman rightly dividing the word of truth.

As a priest we need an example. Our high priest taught his inheritance from the pages of the Old Testament. Of the abundance of the letter, it is written of me. That is our high priest's testimony found in the book of Hebrews. Our guide to inheriting our priesthood.

The Old Testament is the New Testament concealed.

The New Testament is the Old Testament revealed.

Begin a relationship with Messiah today through prayer and supplication with thanksgiving. Open the pages of the Bible daily and see if God does not begin to reveal His will for your life. As a priest we need both testaments to understand the calling on our lives to be a royal priesthood descended from Messiah our Jewish high priest.

He was crucified upon a cross of wood, yet he created the hill upon which it stood.

Even so come Lord Jesus Christ.

John Burns 10-10-2021.

Thou Hast a Few Names

The final warning to the reformation church that birthed denominations, dogma, and doctrines of demons, is that through it all God has reserved a true remnant of believers in the whole plan of God.

Revelation 3:1-6 Unto the Angel of the Church of Sardis

The writer of Revelation gives us the call to repentance found in 1 John 5:4. To be an overcomer.

For whatsoever is born of God overcometh the world: and this is the victory that overcometh the world, even our faith.

Who is he that overcometh the world, but he that believeth that Jesus Christ is the son of God?

This is he that came by water and blood, even Jesus Christ: not by water only but by water and blood. And it is the Spirit that beareth witness, because the Spirit is truth.

For there are three that bear record in heaven, the Father, the Word, and the Holy Ghost: and these three are one.

And there are three that bear witness in earth, the spirit, the water, and the blood. And these three agree in one.

If we receive the witness of men, the witness of God is greater: for this is the witness of God which he has testified of his son. He that believeth on the Son of God has the witness in himself: He that believeth not God has made him a liar.

A person that reads the newspaper knows what is going on in the world. He that reads the whole Bible, understands why!

Religion in any form has a person worship the opinion of the preacher without ever questioning them according to what we are reading in the Bible. Most never open the Bible for themselves, to the detriment of their children, our communities, and our extended families on earth. The Bible was written to every person born of a woman for reproof and correction of doctrines and dogma.

The two-edged sword of God's Word can only be understood through individual belief in the entire message. Religious leaders collect a wage for preaching just like college professors. They petition government for tax breaks, even when Jesus Christ said render unto Caesar that which is Caesars.

The only person to collect money for the message of Messiah in our Bible was Judas the traitor of Messiah. Our churches look just like the world they were called out of. Incredible wealth being horded by preachers. When the rich young ruler asked Jesus Christ what he must do to be saved, Jesus Christ replied, sell everything, give to the poor, and come follow me!

I live in a county with incredible potential to fulfill God's will for America. Southern Christian heritage is hanging on by a thread. God alone can weave a beautiful tapestry from a single thread. He has maintained a remnant of Jewish and Christian believers without the need for denominational bondage.

God does not judge by outward expression of acts of piety. God does not judge a single human by what they do. He only judges by your conviction of what he alone did on Calvary. Your belief in what God was willing to do for you and your testimony to a fallen world of belief in it, will lead to seeing the world through the eyes of God.

God's eyes are tuned to only mercy and grace!

If it were not so, God would have already judged America and that judgement would have occurred in denominational churches first. They left their first love a long time ago in favor of judging others, doctrines found in the Law that God dealt the death blow to on Calvary, and outward appearance over inward conviction.

Is God only saving people that have gone under water baptism? Was the thief Christ promised to meet in paradise water baptized?

Would God speak in any other tongue than Hebrew? What language did Messiah speak while tabernacling with men?

Does God still hate any form of church hierarchy as identified by Jesus Christ as the Nicolaitans?

Does God need mediators between himself and men? Can God get us a message without the need of three-dimensional spaces we wrongly identify with the word church? God gave the Hebrews the temple as an appeasement for asking him to allow them to be like the pagan nations they were called out of. God does not dwell in houses made with human hands. His desire is to inhabit you as the individual to empower you to take the message of mercy and grace to our families, friends, and communities.

Who was John the Baptist according to scripture?

He was a Levite. He was descended from Aaron. He is the authorized high priest at the time of Messiah's advent. His father served in the temple as a priest. He is authorized to accept Messiah as king and priest of a better covenant. He is the voice of one crying in the wilderness in the power of Elijah. He was murdered by Herod the Edomite as part of the plan to shift the priesthood onto the shoulders of Messiah. He ended the need for immersion in water for Messiah was turning water to blood as noted by his first miracle. No one puts new wine into old wineskins!

Jesus Christ corrected John the Baptist's theology. John thought he should be water baptized by Messiah. Jesus Christ corrected him. I must be baptized by you to fulfill all righteousness! What the law could not do, Messiah did in correcting the doctrine John thought Messiah would continue.

Did Jesus Christ baptize anyone in water?

Did Paul who was given the message to take to the gentiles baptize anyone?

Paul was a Jewish pharisee. He was water baptized to finish the need for immersion in water, for Paul came preaching immersion in the blood of the Lamb cleansing us from all unrighteousness. Jesus Christ came by water and blood to fulfill the need for a Levitical priesthood.

If you are going to require gentiles to be water baptized, make sure you require them to keep the entire law with its 613 commands. Be careful you do not convert gentiles to Judaism in your haste to preach only out of the New Testament.

Greek hermeneutics permeates Christian worship in America. Jesus Christ preached using Hebrew hermeneutics for he is a Jewish rabbi. Western preachers separate Messiah from his inheritance as our authorized high priest each time they require a gentile to go under the water. They do it to hold onto whatever market share they currently control. God is not in those churches! There is no power!

Was the Holy Spirit water baptized?

If Messiah is the second person of the creation Godhead and he was water baptized, should not the Bible instruct us on the baptism of water over the Holy Spirit?

Or did the Holy Spirit replace the need for immersion in water for the Holy Spirit speaks to inward conviction while water baptism pleases men seeking outward expression. They want you to look like them not Messiah. Will they recognize Messiah when he returns?

He was crucified upon a cross of wood yet he created the hill upon which it stood!

Even so come Lord Jesus Christ!

John Burns 11-05-2021 RLTW.

Leviticus 25:10

When I am confronted by Americans who always ask about my service in the Rangers while deployed to Somalia, I always tell them the reason I served, not how a firefight went. Those moments are reserved for time spent alone with the people I shared the experience with.

Proclaim liberty throughout the land! How many Americans really understand what was being proclaimed and written on the Liberty Bell in Philadelphia in 1751?

William Penn had chartered the first Pennsylvania constitution in 1701. This was a Jubilee year according to the Bible and how God keeps time.

Penn was a forward-thinking Quaker. Persecution from within the Church had led Puritans to board the Mayflower with Jews by their side and sailed across the Atlantic. The Mayflower compact was the first document written and signed by people who would one day call themselves Americans.

In that compact, the Pilgrims and Jews agreed that the Bible would be the book that decided how they interacted with each other and any indigenous peoples they were to encounter. This is the true foundational statement that would guide Penn in chartering Pennsylvania's first constitution known as the charter of privileges.

In this document we discover that religious liberty was going to be assured for every citizen. Liberal relations would be had with Native Americans. Every citizen would have a say in drafting our laws. This is true Liberalism that Washington, Jefferson, and Adams all believed in.

The Liberty Bell was ordered by the Pennsylvania delegates and delivered in 1751 and housed at the forgery of Pass and Stow. It was the year of the Shemitah. The 7-year agricultural year cycle found in Leviticus 25 was established in our land in the city of Philadelphia in Pennsylvania. America was now following an ancient rule established by God while Israel wondered in the desert.

Revelation 3:1-6 Unto the Angel of the Church of Sardis

St. Paul's Episcopal Church is where we travel next. It is the site where George Washington prayed after delivering our country's first inaugural address. It is where Washington attended church while our nation's first capitol was New York City. He took the oath of office with his hand on the Bible!

This chapel would prove to endure even the terrorist attacks of 9/11/2001. It was Elul 23 on the Hebrew calendar and it was a Shemitah year.

Outside the tabernacle on the world trade center site stood the sycamore tree planted by George Washington as a symbol of our nation's devotion to the God of Abraham, Isaac, Jacob and Joseph. It was damaged in the attacks and was replaced under the administration of Barak Obama with an Erez tree. A white spruce. Is this coincidence?

On Tuesday, September 12, 2001, the leader of the Democratic party and majority leader in the United States Senate issued a rebuke to the terrorists who had attacked us. Within his remarks he quoted Isaiah 9 Vs. 10 and 11. It reads the bricks have fallen but we shall rebuild with hewn stone. The sycamore has been felled but we shall plant an Erez tree. This statement in Isaiah God viewed as a statement of pride, for Israel did not recognize that God had allowed the Assyrian terrorists destroy the Northern kingdom in Israel as a warning to his covenant people.

Was God warning America when he allowed the same terrorists speaking the language of ancient Assyria to attack his covenant people in America? On Elul 29, the closing of the Shemitah year in 2001, the stock market lost 3.37% of its value. God was sending a message to those he loves! It was 9-18-2001 on our western calendar.

Has the Shemitah manifest since in America? Have the ancient harbingers of judgement manifest in America? 2008 saw the Shemitah manifest under George Bush the economy of the world lost 2 trillion dollars in liquid capitol. Lehman brothers our nation's 5th largest bank collapsed while our leaders answer was to double down, print more money, pick which institutions would fail and the pattern of Judgement continued still with no repentance by Americans in Churches and synagogues. It all occurred in the year and final week of the Shemitah year. By the time the fall was over, the market had lost 777 points. Coincidence?

Enter 2015 and the Presidency of Barak Obama. He is a friend to all things Muslim and all things dealing with the worship of Nebo and the Moon God. The house of the moon God worship began in Jericho, and now we are immigrating moon worshippers here in large numbers. Does the Bible support this in a nation dedicated to the God of the Bible?

On August 18, 2015 which was the beginning of the last month of the Shemitah year. It was the third of Elul. By the 29th of Elul that year the stock market had gone on its wildest ride in history but not the crash we would expect the paradigm to follow. Why?

This Shemitah year of 2015 was the 49th year of the pattern of 7 times 7 years established as the year before the jubilee was proclaimed. 2016 was the jubilee year. The 29th of Elul which closes out the Sabbath of years was October 2. Pride had filled America and the memory of the 9/11 warnings were fading fast. God sent America a judge in the form of Donald Trump.

This too follows the pattern of King Jehu dealing the death blow to the house of Ahab and Jezebel. Trump would win the election. The party in power went about destroying his presidency but not for the reasons the news reported. The Russian hoax was launched by those trying to stop God's plan for America and the world.

Trump did something no president before had the courage to do: He named Jerusalem the eternal capital of Israel. He began to negotiate with the Sunni Muslim countries Daniel identifies as the ten toes of Nebuchadnezzars statue. Three signed on to legitimize relations with Israel. Now they had to stop him for he was doing the bidding of God and the Bible alone identifies Trump as a modern manifestation of King Jehu. He will be back and the Bible says so!

He was crucified upon a cross of wood yet he created the hill upon which it stood. Even so come Lord Jesus Christ. We are currently in the Shemitah year of 2022. What will September reveal in God's plan?

John Burns RLTW, 08 November 2021.

The Shmita

Rosh Hashanna is the beginning of the new year on the calendar Jesus Christ followed. It begins at sundown on

Tishre 1. It is referred to as the head of months, for it is the beginning of the Hebrew civil year.

2021 ended in Israel on Elul 29 which was September 6. The new Shmita year began at sundown on September 7, 2021. Does it mean anything for Christians in America?

The month of Elul in the year 2022 begins at sundown on August 28. Elul 29 is September 25, 2022. Let's see if God has anything planned for America and the world?

I suspect being the first Shmita after the Jubilee of 2016, and the nation's rejection at the polls of Donald Trump, will lead to I believe, the American dollar completely collapsing, and the pattern of harbingers manifesting in America will continue.

America will be bankrupt, and Donald Trump is the only former president to emerge from bankruptcy, more prosperous than when it happened in his life. America will need Trump to bring us into the messianic age.

Now you know why the Democratic party and the Godless liberals in the Republican party united to allow the FBI and our State Department, to weaponize and stop him from draining the swamp they inhabit. They are united to stop the Biblical plan of God!

Is there any other Hebrew holidays Jesus Christ followed when he walked the earth that have anything to do with the true church Jesus Christ intends to marry?

Jesus Christ went to the temple to celebrate the feast of Dedication. Today it is referred to as Hannukah. Why would Jesus Christ celebrate Hannukah?

Revelation 3:1-6 Unto the Angel of the Church of Sardis

Hannukah is the feast when Jews gather to light the 7 golden candlesticks of Dedication. The Jews do it to remember the second temple that was re-dedicated after the Maccabean revolt. This is the Usurper King Herod's Temple.

I personally believe the true temple Jesus Christ was going to dedicate during the feast of Hannukah before his crucifixion was the temple of his earthly body. I also believe he was pointing the Jews toward the millennial temple that Messiah returns to after the Jews look upon him whom they have pierced, and cry hosannah, blessed is he who comes in the name of the Lord.

Zechariah prophesied of this event at the end of the seven-year tribulation. It is reserved for interaction by God to chasten the nation he birthed in Egypt for the last time. It is the same time period the bride of Christ is in heaven receiving her prophesied crowns. It is identified by God as the time of Jacob's trouble.

What precedes the seven-year tribulation of the last days? Is it the time identified by Messiah as the times of the Gentiles? How does the times of the Gentiles end? Is the bride the object of Messiah's affection during this age? Has it been going on for 2,000 years? Is it almost over?

Jesus Christ referred to his church as the seven golden lampstands. In Hebrew, the church is the menorah of Israel. They just do not recognize it at this time and most Christians believe God replaced Israel with his Church. That is not what the Bible says. Eugenic minded Christian preachers have segregated us into denominations where the entire Bible is not studied. If it were, I would not have to be teaching this lesson from our God now.

In Revelation 1-3 the Church identified as the seven lampstands is on earth experiencing the times of the gentiles. In Revelation 4 the believers are in Heaven receiving their vestures as priests and their crowns as Kings, thus beginning Daniel's 70th week on Earth. The times of Jacob's trouble.

For the mystery of iniquity doth already work: only he who now letteth shall, let until he be taken out of the way. Who is a he who now letteth that if taken out of the way would end the times of the gentiles? It is a he and he is also identified as the restrainer. Might it be the Holy Spirit?

If the Holy Spirit were removed from the earth is there a mechanism for people to come to Christ? Our guide is Stephen. He was Martyred for his testimony of saving faith in Messiah. If you enter the final seven years of gentile government on Earth your only chance for salvation is martyrdom. The body of Christ will persecute Jews and once again confiscate their property.

The Shmita of 2022 ends at sundown on September 25. The feast of trumpets is September 26. Is this coincidence or do trumpets serve a purpose for our God?

Four things are recognized by God on the feast of Trumpets. It is the day of judgement when Jews ask for forgiveness. It is also the day of remembrance when Jews remember the history of their people. It is New Year's Day to the Jew and our Messiah. Most importantly to Christians it is the day the shofar is blown.

The shofar is the root word for esophagus, the very trumpet by which God asks every person born of a woman to worship him as creator. We are all without excuse. Let everything that has breath praise the Lord. He gave you your very own trumpet with which to witness to a fallen world and what are we doing with it?

Judging others while not acknowledging the sin in our own eyes which so easily ensnares us?

Gossiping about people not present to defend themselves?

Singing everything but the praises of our God?

How does the feast of trumpets line up with the Bible narrative?

God tells Jesus Christ to retrieve his beloved from all the nations of the earth at the sound of the trumpet. Messiah comes in the clouds to receive his promised reward for enduring the cross. They return to heaven to celebrate the marriage supper of the Lamb which lasts seven years! The bride is in heaven while the rest of the world endures the tribulation.

Are you a virgin bride eagerly awaiting the return of the bridegroom to receive you unto himself? Have you worshipped the gods of this world and kept the Roman religious calendar in your church? I am the Lord your God you shall have no other gods before me. Will God compromise for our pitiful sake? I think not.

He was crucified upon a cross of wood yet he created the hill upon which it stood.

Even so come Lord Jesus Christ.

John Burns 11-7-2021.

Revelation 3:7-13 Unto the Angel of the Church of Philadelphia

7 And to the angel of the church in Philadelphia write; These things saith he that is holy, he that is true, he that hath the key of David, he that openeth, and no man shutteth; and shutteth, and no man openeth; ⁸ I know thy works: behold, I have set before thee an open door, and no man can shut it: for thou hast a little strength, and hast kept my word, and hast not denied my name. ⁹ Behold, I will make them of the synagogue of Satan, which say they are Jews, and are not, but do lie; behold, I will make them to come and worship before thy feet, and to know that I have loved thee. ¹⁰ Because thou hast kept the word of my patience, I also will keep thee from the hour of temptation, which shall come upon all the world, to try them that dwell upon the earth. ¹¹ Behold, I come quickly: hold that fast which thou hast, that no man take thy crown. ¹² Him that overcometh will I make a pillar in the temple of my God, and he shall go no more out: and I will write upon him the name of my God, and the name of the city of my God, which is new Jerusalem, which cometh down out of heaven from my God: and I will

write upon him my new name. ¹³ He that hath an ear, let him hear what the Spirit saith unto the churches.

The Missionary Church

Messiah has now dictated five letters to John with each having certain qualities and certain problems. Philadelphia is one of two churches that has nothing bad said about it by Messiah. Is this church alive today?

Philadelphia is a feminine pronoun. It is made from two Greek words. Philo is friendly. Delphia is a city in western Turkey at the crossroads of Greek culture and Roman conquest. It was a strategic city at the time of John the Revelator.

It was the wine producing region of the pro-consulate of Asia minor at the time of Christ. The Greek God Dionysius was being venerated, and it was an incredibly wealthy community. Christian missionary outreach began in Philadelphia to the Gentile world.

Jesus Christ introduces us to a term found in Isaiah 22. It is the key to the house of David. What does it mean?

David was chosen King by God long before he was born. His life is one of incredible valor, incredible peril, and incredible intemperance. Yet, he is the only man in the Bible God identifies as a man after his own heart. In both the New Testament and Old Testament. What is the key to his house?

We are introduced to Eliakim the scribe. His name transliterates into English as God raises up. He is the son of Hilkiah, the man appointed over the King's treasury under

Hezekiah. David removes Shibna for the purpose of making Eliakim his treasurer over the house of Judah. Is this a Biblical paradigm playing out in the Church of Philadelphia?

With great wealth comes tremendous responsibility to those around us in the kingdom of our God. Hoarding wealth was the reason David removed Shibna and replaced him with Eliakim. At the time of the advent of Messiah, the high priest with the Pharisees and Sadducees were selling the message of salvation and hoarding tremendous wealth. Is that happening today in Church?

America became the envy of the world. With that envy came incredible missionary outreach. No nation on Earth sent more missionaries around the world than America. We became a nation that shared like no other, and God blessed us. We are the only nation on Earth to boast of a middle class. That middle class was built on the backs of Jews and Christians who believed in tithing and missionary outreach. Have they disappeared?

Shibna had begun to forgo the laws God established for the Jews in the Exodus. The Shmita was not being kept and the poor in Israel were suffering. The tithe was not being applied to feeding the poor with the first 10% of Israel's increase. They had begun to worship the two golden calves of military might and monetary strength. They were forgoing thus says the Lord in order to look like the world they were called out of, just like America today.

Jesus Christ introduces us to Philadelphia as a Church that he is fully in. He is the door which no man shutteth or openeth.

He is the way, the truth, and the life, not their own ability to create and collect wealth. He is the provider of prosperity from which we are to share and not hoard. The missionary church identified as Messiah's bride who will not go through the tribulation. He knows her works and he loves them.

This church has kept his entire word. As a Jewish Rabbi, that meant living the entire Bible. Christ is the subject of John's revelation. Jesus Christ as God, is who is being revealed and doing the blessing and administering the admonishments found in five churches in five letters. He is holding the door open which no man can shut. In Laodicea, he will be standing at the door wanting back in to their church experience, and missionary outreach is how he intends to establish who his true bride is.

God created everything money can buy. Why do we worship our own ability to hoard wealth and earn income? Why do men forgo the worship of God as provider, in favor of thinking he needs help providing for us? To learn to trust God as provider of all things monetary is the key to becoming a missionary outreach church.

Giving should never be done out of abundance but out of your need to fulfill God's will for his creation. Money has become the foundation by which nations fight wars. Natural resources are how they value currency. Every geopolitical decision is made by nations for the hoarding and consumption of the resources God created. They are his not ours. What a Christian does with his or her money matters to God. He blesses you with prosperity for the sole purpose of achieving his goals for building the kingdom.

Jesus Christ was asked by the rich young ruler what must I do to be saved? Christ's answer: sell everything, give to the poor, and come follow me. We never hear from him again in the scriptures. What will you hold onto more than Jesus' command to help the poor? Do you worship what moth and rust decay? Are your things more important than your relationship to Messiah?

America was brought into existence by a loving God for the purpose of showing the world the cross and the God who bore our burdens upon it. Philadelphia is the place our founders gave us a government of, for, and by the people. Have we as a people fulfilled God's will for the world he desires to save?

Missionary outreach must once again become a critical part of our Christian experience. Tithing as taught by our Jewish ancestors found in the Old Testament must be rightly understood and rightly practiced if you intend to be blessed by God in your ministry. Malachi explains God's idea for tithing, and Genesis 12 identifies who we should bless with our missionary outreach. Return to tithing and giving to the poor and God will bless your church in ways you do not see coming.

Remember: No one can beat God at giving. He gave us his son to pay the only debt that matters when we die: our sin debt to God as creator.

He was crucified upon a cross of wood, yet he created the hill upon which it stood.

Even so come Lord Jesus Christ.

John Burns 11-22-2021 RLTW.

The Synagogue of Satan

Who is Jesus Christ referring to as people who are Jews in name only? The misunderstood question on church history and all because Satan got into church way back in Ephesus. They lost their first love as Jews who believed in Messiah. Was John the Revelator Jewish? Was Messiah a Jewish rabbi? Then who are the Jews in name only?

Western pastors have gone to Greek seminaries and practiced Greek interpretation techniques with a Jewish book called our Bible. The term coined is eugenics. It permeates every aspect of our lives to include how we perceive God's Word.

Eugenics is born when a preacher believes he is better than anyone in his flock when it comes to interpreting the Bible. It is his way, or, the highway model being taught, not Jesus Christ's way, for he is Jewish, and practices Hebrew interpretation techniques based upon him being the subject of every word of the Bible. He knows better than me or your Bible teacher.

These charlatan preachers separate Jesus Christ from his Jewish future. They tell you western Christianity replaced Jews, yet they practice Jewish religious traditions Messiah fulfilled as a Jewish high priest and Jewish king awaiting his coming kingdom on earth.

They require you to be placed under the Hebrew Mikveh ceremonial cleansing through immersion in water to prove you are as saved as them. Even though Jesus Christ changed water to wine at his first miracle, the wedding supper at Cana.

Wine is indicative of the blood of the Lamb cleansing us from all unrighteousness. Water baptism prepares you as a gentile for deodorant and nothing more. Jesus Christ fulfilled the need for the High priest to be immersed in water and he reminded John the Baptist he was replacing the need for water with the requirement to be covered in the blood of the Lamb.

Water does not save you from one sin. And you become a Jew in name only when you require people to get under the water and not the blood. You are serving at the synagogue of Satan.

It pains me to have to teach this to people that are comfortable doing what their ancestors did. Continuing in church tradition rather than finding out if what I am saying is true according to the entire Bible.

These men are leading many astray by clinging to tradition more than accepting the entire testimony of the Bible. Antisemitism is at the heart of what I am saying. Racism, classism, sexism, socialism all point to the Greek model of interpretation practiced by modern American eugenicists found on every corner of our America.

1 John 2:27 states that we have an anointing from God, we do not need any of these men to include me to teach you. Acts 17:11 says the Bereans searched the scripture daily to find out if what Paul were saying is true?

Do you rely on pastors, preachers and teachers for your spiritual growth? They will not be there with you when you stand before the Lord and receive your just recompense for those things having done in the flesh.

Jesus Christ desires a personal relationship to him as Messiah. We must all fast and pray to find out if what the entire Bible says is true. You cannot separate one word from the message or it becomes a cult!

Jesus Christ said no scripture is available for individual interpretation. Isaiah 28 teaches us God spread his true message across the breadth of the entire Bible. Here a little, there a little. He is keeping Satan off guard not believers, this is why we need Holy Spirit anointing in each of our lives. I love to debate the entire Word of God. It is my story of saving faith in Messiah and he is a coming Jewish king!

Christ's humility had to replace my ability in all things scriptural. I had a lot of baggage when God rescued me from myself and began to save me. It began with the space between my own ears and has continued for 43 years and counting since I first pondered the question: Did God say?

I have experienced a lot of death in my life. I have buried 40 friends in military cemeteries all across America. I have lost an infant brother, but none hurt more than when I buried my granddaughter after she died in my arms while doing CPR. Religion became my refuge. I stuck to what my grandparents did and attended every denomination of church in America. None could assuage the hurt I felt over losing my baby girl.

I asked God "If you are who the Bible says you are, then show me?" I began to study the Bible first by losing all of my pre-suppositions I had learned while attending every church. The journey has been long and God has been faithful to me the greatest of sinners. I had to leave eugenics I learned in western denominational churches and take every word of the Bible literally. I was tired of being a Jew in name only. God instructed me to believe I was a new creation and old things had to pass away. None more than religious conviction!

Did God write the Bible to every person born of a woman or just to certain men who then tell us what it says? I am sticking with the Trinity to achieve the goals he has for my life. Doctrines of men hold no sway over my life. God provides me with mercy and grace and that is what I offer every person I come in contact with. I shame no one into belief in Messiah by charging them as sinners, that is God's job to convict a person and I can save no one.

Philadelphia is the place God intended to establish missionary outreach in America in the homes of Messiah's friends. Those homes are where people are once again being saved with no need for churches who practice Jewish doctrines. God is in control and Messiah is calling his bride home!

He was crucified upon a cross of wood, yet he created the hill upon which it stood.

Even so come Lord Jesus Christ.

John Burns 11-22-2021 RLTW.

The Hour of Temptation

What hour is Jesus Christ speaking of?

According to Daniel the hour of temptation is a specific seven-year period that is titled the time of Jacob's trouble. It is the 70th week missing from chapter 9 of the book of Daniel. It fits exactly with the period identified by Jesus Christ that begins in Revelation chapter 4 verse 1. Christians must answer the question "Do I believe the entire Bible or do I just cling to what my preacher tells me about my salvation?"

In Revelation 3 we are introduced to the word THE. In Greek it is the word EK. It is a definite article that shows possession. It is a very specific hour with very specific purposes outlined in scripture by our God. It takes the mouths of two or more witnesses to understand our condition as pertaining to this 7-year period of time.

Christians are never identified as Jacob or his descendants in the flesh. We are grafted into the living vine begun with Adam and traveling through the 42 generations of men identified by the writers of Matthew and Luke. It is a living vine with living members who are indeed Jewish. The vine is Messiah and he is indeed a descendant of Jacob in his flesh. He alone is qualified to judge the people known as the descendants of Jacob.

Revelation 3:7-13 Unto the Angel of the Church of Philadelphia

The time identified by Jesus Christ as the hour of temptation is also called the tribulation of the last 7 years of gentile government on earth. It is broke-down into two periods of time, each equaling 3 and ½ years on a Babylonian calendar of 360-day years. It is identified as a time, times and half a time. It is also identified in scripture as 2 periods each totaling 1,260 days each.

The tribulation will see the majority of the body of Christ have only martyrdom to turn to. They have not eagerly awaited the bridegroom's return. They cling to Roman religious traditions begun by church leaders during the 2,000-period known as the times of the Gentiles.

That time period ends with the church of Laodicea. It is identified as the Apostate church that needs not the blood of the Lamb cleansing them from all unrighteousness. They have their Roman pagan feast days and Christian witness is furthest from their minds.

Traditions of men replaced thus says the Lord and they have no intention of changing. They have money, power, and willing church members to stay on the wide road leading to destruction with them. I pray for these members of the body of Christ daily to receive Holy Spirit conviction and repent and return to the Bible for all matters concerning our future as professing Christians.

I love America and I love Americans. I have deployed to war zones to defend the freedoms we all enjoy. I was wounded in war, and returned to an America stuck in ancestor worship, Roman beliefs, and abject scorn toward all things outlined in scripture.

At the heart of the matter, Christian eugenics taught at western seminary that denies 87% of scripture in favor of holding on to our extremely pagan church liturgy schedule. Will God negotiate with these churches when he returns, I think not.

What is the remedy offered by Messiah to the churches?

1 John 5:4 identifies our means by which we must become overcomers in the flesh. To believe that Messiah died, was buried, and rose again the third day. This is our only means by which a condemned sinner is justified before a holy and righteous God. We cannot add any human tradition to our proclamation of faith. Just ask the thief on the cross? He is in paradise because he recognized he was guilty and Jesus Christ was not! No water baptism here. He was baptized with Messiah's true baptism identified by Matthew in chapter 20 of his gospel.

The baptism Jesus Christ identified is the one he was to be baptized with on Calvary and the true baptism every Christian must be willing to endure, if we are truly saved. It has nothing to do with water and everything to do with blood! That is why Jesus Christ identifies this true baptism days before he was crucified and three years after he went under the Mikveh baptism requirement for Jewish high priests identified by God when he ordered Aaron to be water baptized in the book of Exodus. It is a Jewish baptism that solves none of your sin issues.

How many professing Christians are truly willing to endure persecution to the point of death? Matthew 20 identifies Jesus Christ as saying if you are not willing to die and receive my one true baptism identified by Paul as a second witness, then you are not worthy to enter my coming kingdom.

It is a baptism of blood, so take up your cross daily and come follow Messiah as he allowed himself to be crucified to human tradition and endured the cross!

What awaits a person willing to endure persecution for the testimony of salvation alone in Messiah's death, burial, and resurrection? The crown of righteousness. The first crown is on the house, the rest of the crowns revolve around what we do with our testimony.

Messiah alone is our coming Jewish King. I have devoted my entire adult life to teaching the truths of the entire Bible because I love you! I have nothing to gain and I accept no money for the message Jesus Christ freely gave me.

I desire to rule and reign with Messiah in his coming kingdom. He has accepted my testimony of faith leading to the crucifixion of my own religious beliefs which could never save me. I am his bride and I eagerly await the return of my bridegroom.

He was crucified upon a cross of wood, yet he created the hill upon which it stood.

He is alive forevermore and he is returning for his true virgin bride very soon.

I love you all.

In Christ's eternal service, John Burns. 12- 10-2021

Revelation 3:14-22 Unto the Angel of the Church of Laodicea

14 And unto the angel of the church of the Laodiceans write; These things saith the Amen, the faithful and true witness, the beginning of the creation of God; ¹⁵ I know thy works, that thou art neither cold nor hot: I would thou wert cold or hot. ¹⁶ So then because thou art lukewarm, and neither cold nor hot, I will spue thee out of my mouth. ¹⁷ Because thou sayest, I am rich, and increased with goods, and have need of nothing; and knowest not that thou art wretched, and miserable, and poor, and blind, and naked: ¹⁸ I counsel thee to buy of me gold tried in the fire, that thou mayest be rich; and white raiment, that thou mayest be clothed, and that the shame of thy nakedness does not appear; and anoint thine eyes with eye-salve, that thou mayest see. ¹⁹ As many as I love, I rebuke and chasten: be zealous therefore, and repent. ²⁰ Behold, I stand at the door, and knock: if any man, hear my voice, and open the door, I will come in to him, and will sup with him, and he with me. ²¹ To him that overcometh will I grant to sit with me in my throne, even as I also overcame, and am set down with my

Father in his throne. ²² He that hath an ear, let him hear what the Spirit saith unto the churches.

Christ's Letter to Laodicea

And to the angel of the church of the Laodiceans write: These things sayeth the Amen, the faithful and true witness, the beginning of the creation of God: I know thy works, that thou aren't neither cold or hot.

So then because thou art lukewarm, I will spue thee out of my mouth.

Because thou sayest, I am rich and increased with goods, and have need of nothing: and knowest not that thou art wretched, and miserable, and poor, and blind, and naked: I counsel thee to buy of me gold tried in the fire, that thou mayest be rich, and white raiment: that thou mayest be clothed, and that the shame of thy nakedness does not appear: and anoint thine eyes with eye-salve, that thou mayest see.

As many as I love I rebuke and chasten: be zealous therefore and repent.

Behold I stand at the door, and knock: If any man, hear my voice, and, open the door, I will come into him, and will sup with him, and he with me.

To him that over-cometh will I grant to sit with me in my throne, even as I overcame, and am set down with my father, in his throne.

He that hath an ear, let him hear what the Spirit says to the churches. Revelation 3; Vs. 14-22.

This letter is Christ's letter to the apostate church which epitomizes what went wrong over 2,000 years of Christian history. The Apostolic church in Ephesus saw Messiah's first disciples believe he was Israel's messiah. All they wanted to do was spend time alone with Jesus Christ as he showed them, he was indeed, the word who became flesh and tabernacled amongst us.

The four Gospels outline the history of Messiah and his time sojourning in our world and all for the purpose of dying, not living. He is the only man in history born knowing exactly who, what, where, when, and why about his own physical death and resurrection.

He called the apostles in eternity past, and knew them all by name at creation. John was the last living witness to Messiah's ministry who founded the seven churches Jesus Christ has chosen to identify as prophetic to church history.

Ephesus is where John planted Apostolic seeds in western Turkey. From Ephesus, the Gospel would travel to the four corners of the earth, during the gentile church age. It was in Ephesus where men started a Church hierarchy against the wishes of God.

The apostles had begun to forgo spending time alone with Messiah in prayer and the study of scripture, for Church attendance. The buildings they inhabited became more important than the Messiah who died for them. Christ has always desired personal relationship over church attendance.

Smyrna began with the martyrdom of Paul and Peter under Emperor Nero. Ten specific Roman emperors would issue decrees ordering the execution of people of the way. These were Jews who accepted Messiah's testimony, and, gentiles who had the mystery of Jesus Christ's kingdom revealed to them in Philippians. The gentiles would be fellow-heirs with the Jewish believers in Messiah.

To escape persecution at the hands of the Roman Government, Christians compromised under Constantine, and married the world at Pergamos. They adopted men as hierarchy over their liturgy schedule and these men in turned combined Roman paganism with a little bit of Jesus on Sunday.

At Thyatira an ancient paradigm appeared in the middle age Catholic church. Ahab and Jezebel became the pattern of Roman bishops confiscating property after murdering Jews and Christians. Inquisitions gave way to the holocaust of World War II. The denial of Jesus Christ's Jewish past, and his entirely Jewish future is what was adopted as doctrine in Thyatira.

Sardis was where men began to want the Bible back in their homes. Denominations were spurned throughout the Lutheran reformation, each with their own ideas of interpreting scripture. Luther did nothing to correct the Romanization of our liturgy schedule, thus, it was at Sardis that the Church died.

Philadelphia saw believers desire to build a country where Jesus Christ was the God of the Bible. We prospered when we sent missionaries around the world. That prosperity led to incredible compromise right here in America. America gave birth to the modern church of Laodicea.

In the Colossian letter, they are instructed by Paul to exchange letters with the Laodiceans. Apparently, they both were experiencing the same problems Messiah looked to correct.

The Colossians had begun to not accept the deity of Jesus Christ. They had turned to knowledge and away from the true fear of the Lord. They were interpreting scripture using Greek hermeneutics.

Everyone has their own self relativism. Thus says the Lord was exchanged for human traditions of men. They clung to all of their ancestors' pre-suppositions about salvation, and church became more important than personal relationship to Messiah.

Now, Messiah is outside of their three-dimensional buildings that God says he does not dwell in. They have increased with goods, they have need of nothing, and men rule their hearts, not Jesus Christ.

Government as God is what they have accepted, and God no longer supplies all of their needs according to his riches in glory. They are lukewarm, and gather in vain without ever offering Messiah to a world outside of their denominational structure.

Jesus Christ stands at the door and knocks. He is wanting back in to every person, in every church's heart, and, he desires that you make him Lord of your life by returning to every word of scripture from Genesis to Revelation. Will you answer the still soft voice of God and repent and return to scripture literacy?

We have entered the Laodicean church age which ends with the catching away of Messiah's bride and the beginning of Daniel's 70th week. It is the times of Jacob's trouble reserved for the chastening of the Jewish people in Israel and around the world. The bride of Christ will be removed and Laodicea does not share her future with Messiah.

The Lord Jesus Christ had nothing good to say about Laodicea. The time is short. Will you listen to the Holy Spirit as he tells you God desires your reproof and correction, and the Bible is required for you to understand our predicament?

He was crucified upon a cross of wood, yet he created the hill upon which it stood. Return to the death, burial, and resurrection of Jesus Christ for your salvation from the sin that so easily ensnares us all. Mercy is needed in Christian Church so grace can appear in America again!

John Burns RLTW 12-23-2021.

I Hate Divorce

The first covenant in the Bible is found in Genesis 2:24. For this reason shall a man leave his mother and father, and cleave unto the bosom of his wife, and the two shall become one flesh.

This covenant sets the tone for the entire Bible narrative. It is framed behind the writing prose that God is married to his creation. The Father is married to national Israel. The Son is betrothed to a Gentile bride the Holy Spirit has been finding him for 1968 years and counting. The Terra Firma is being redeemed as a product of God's Love for his creation.

Laodicea is an interesting character in Bible history. In Daniel Chapter 11 we are introduced to the abomination that causes desolation. A world leader from the Greek house of Seleucus, has sacked Egypt and enraged the Senate in Rome. Antiochus Epiphanes is a Type of Anti-Christ we encounter in Daniel's prophecies.

Rome sends a Senator to confront Antiochus in Egypt concerning his plans for the Roman territory. He draws a line in the sand and demands an answer before he leaves the circle in the Egyptian sand. His wife is a Greek woman of the house of Laodicea. Her name means rule by the people.

Antiochus abandons his endeavor and begins the trek back to his lands in western Turkey. He decides to sack Jerusalem and subjugate the Jewish nation to retaliate for his losses in Egypt and to taunt fledgling Rome. The Year is 168 BC.

He sets up a statue to the Greek god Zeus, and sacrifices a sow on the altar in the holy of holies in Jerusalem. This is the first abomination that causes desolation in history. It leads to the Maccabean revolt, and the appointment of the Herod's as vassal kings in Jerusalem.

Antiochus divorces Laodicea but not before building her a pagan Greek city at the crossroads of the fledgling Roman empire in western Turkey. Laodicea was at the center of commerce in Asia minor and had become renowned for its hot springs found throughout its territory. This is where the church earned the moniker lukewarm.

Is Laodicea the place God finally gets fed up and divorces the organized church?

Why does the church expect tax breaks while following an American business model? Today's denominational church looks exactly like the world they have been called out of. They own property, provide their pastor a salary that will eventually burden his flock with a pension he believes he is owed. Jesus Christ prophesied that we are to render unto Caesar that which is Caesar's. Money is a mechanism for pagan government not Christianity.

During the Laodicean church age, American preachers educated at western seminaries began to teach money as seed. Give me your money as a seed offering and God will provide you with a harvest of more money. God does not need money to get his message of redemption to the fallen world. These men have their only reward from God, it is their greed!

For God will provide all of your needs according to his riches in glory. He is the creator of everything money can buy, that men go mad over. The love of money is the root of all evil. Money has led to American Christians turning their children into covetous beggars on the various Roman holidays Jesus Christ never celebrated.

Courage to believe in Jesus Christ as creator is what is missing most from our faith journey. The first Jewish converts to the new WAY were willing to be persecuted to the point of death for their conviction that the creator of the universe entered his creation for the purpose of dying on the cross to pay your sin debt. Do you understand that it was the creator on that cross?

When the religious leaders of the day, began to try and muzzle the ox while he was treading out the grain, confronted Messiah, based on their own interpretations of the law, Messiah rebuked them. He reminded them that of the abundance of the law it is written of me. Christ is the subject matter of every word of the Bible, not just the new. God built the foundations of the New Testament solely upon the cornerstone of creation found only in the Old Testament.

You have been redeemed by the same Holy Spirit that raised Jesus Christ from the dead. The same Holy Spirit that found the apostles, disciples and every other writer of God's written revealed word, empowers us to become the true KOINONOS or church. It has nothing to do with three dimensional spaces and everything to do with how much time you spend with Jesus Christ as Lord over your life.

God intended miracles to be wrought at the hands of people who confess Jesus Christ as Lord. To deny this fundamental Bible principle is to deny the Holy Spirit that purchased you. This Christian walk is supernatural, yet we let our natural man convince us that God does not desire miracles of healing, the blind seeing, the deaf hearing. These men believe in a form of God, but deny his power.

Christian eugenics is in full throttle here in America. Each denomination believes their doctrines are the way to Messiah. Like the Greek pagans who educate them at seminary, they adopt the well born stock model in Christian church leading to racism, sexism, classism, and socialism. These men do not even realize that they are the ones who have compromised with the fallen world in favor of wealth, property, and possessions.

Very soon Messiah will be told by God to go retrieve your bride. The majority of the body of Christ will then be wondering what went wrong as God fulfills his promise of removing her prior to the tribulation coming upon this world of unbelievers. We are living in the times the Bible says more about than it does the time Messiah walked the streets of Jerusalem.

He was crucified upon a cross of wood yet he created the hill upon which it stood. He is coming to get his bride very soon. Repent and return to the truths of the entire Bible. Your future depends upon your humility leading to repentance.

In Christ's eternal service, John Burns 12-26-2021.

He that Hath an Ear

Jesus Christ ended each letter with a call to homiletic integrity. Each letter he dictated to John he ended with the same quote: He that hath an ear let him hear what the spirit says to the churches.

These seven churches were chosen by Christ to warn every person who ever claimed faith in Messiah that this is the fate of human religion. Doctrines of men replaced sound Hebrew hermeneutics that Messiah actually used when he taught the apostles and disciples.

These seven churches were started by John in western Turkey prior to him being imprisoned on the island of Patmos by Emperor Domitian. John could visibly see the cities where these churches were begun while incarcerated. Jesus Christ chose to address these churches as God incarnate. The Revelation is the unveiling of Messiah as God, and the unveiling of His bride from within the body of Christ.

These letters make up the most complete prophetic warning to those Messiah loves. Will you recognize all of our need to heed Jesus Christ's warning, and become the virgin bride awaiting the return of our risen bridegroom. Do you have an ear that can hear?

If you approach scripture as God dictates then no scripture is available for individual interpretation. Are there other witnesses to what Messiah was teaching about the body and the bride of Christ?

Ephesians enlightened all of us to the fact that the apostles had lost their first love. After being called by Messiah as humble fisherman, tax collectors, shepherds, and carpenters to take the Gospel to the world that then was, they became so busy with the business of church that they had neglected spending time alone with Messiah.

Revelation 3:14-22 Unto the Angel of the Church of Laodicea

Paul penned the letter to the Ephesian Church explaining the weapons of the kingdom of our God. It outlined that God was the God of time and three-dimensional spaces were less important than spending time alone in prayer and meditation, focusing on what Messiah did and not what they were doing. Church became more important than relationship to Messiah as an individual.

Smyrna would see the beginning of joy through human suffering. This is Paul's message outlined in the book of Philippians. Persecution saw the Christian witness move into the fledgling Roman empire. People in Smyrna were willing to be persecuted for their testimony of saving faith in Messiah and Jesus Christ had nothing bad to say about them.

To avoid persecution at the hands of Rome, the Christian church married the world system at Pergamos. Roman calendars replaced the Genesis calendar Jesus Christ followed while on Earth. Pagan traditions emigrated into Christian liturgy schedules and they are still present today. Paul penned 1st and 2nd Corinthians warning of pagan traditions entering the Christian testimony.

At Thyatira we are warned about Ahab and Jezebel. The middle age Catholic Church that engaged in inquisitions to seize Christian and Jewish property in favor of temporal power. The holocaust was a result of silent pulpits compromising with Pagan human government in Germany. Another holocaust is on our American horizon according to Messiah in this warning to his churches. Persecution came from within church and it will continue in America and our world very soon.

Thyatira was where replacement theology became Christian doctrine. The Catholic Church advanced a narrative that God replaced Israel with pagan gentile believers in Roman traditions. The entire pantheon of pagan Roman Gods emigrated into Christian teachings. Antisemitism became the church moniker. It is present today in every denomination and it is unscriptural. Paul the Apostle penned Galatians as the companion witness to Christ's letter to Thyatira. It deals with the question of is God going to save a Jewish remnant of believers in Messiah?

Today, there are 68 messianic Jewish congregations in Israel and thousands in America. This should put to bed this heretical doctrine advanced by Nicolaitans willing to destroy our Christian witness. These men kept the Bible out of the hands of believers in God for a long time in Roman Catholicism. The middle age church of Rome gave birth to the reformation church of Sardis.

In Sardis we are introduced to Martin Luther. A coal miners' son who went to Rome to seek a degree in law. A chance lightning storm scared him so bad, he decided to change his major to theology. The world was introduced to Habbakuk 2:4 and men began to demand access to the Bible in their homes.

We are saved by faith through grace, not by works less any man should boast. The Bible was available to everyone yet still men clung to religious traditions. Messiah warns Sardis that they are a dead church in need of resurrection. This is the denominational church in all of its present forms. Paul penned his letter to the Hebrews to deal with the antisemitism in Sardis and throughout the reformation churches. Paul answers the question who are the Just in Roman's. How shall the Just live, in Galatians, and what is Faith in Hebrews. For the Just shall live by his faith.

Sardis gave birth to the fledgling nation we all call home, America. Philadelphia is the place missionary outreach traveled all over the globe. As America prospered the church sent missionaries around the world and in turn America prospered. Thessalonians was written by Paul as the definitive guide to proper Christian reaction to salvation. The doctrine of the harpazo, referred to as the rapture of the bride of Christ is in Thessalonians.

With the trappings of wealth in Philadelphia we enter the Laodicean church age. America is under the abandonment wrath of God and no one in church needs the blood of the Lamb cleansing them from all unrighteousness, I have money, a church, cars, homes and a Roman calendar to worship God on. That is why Laodicea is the church God intends to divorce. Do you have an ear to hear what the spirit says?

The Laodiceans were told by Paul to exchange letters with the Collossians. Paul penned his letter to Collosse almost 40 years before Messiah dictated the letter to Laodicea. Proving the entire Bible to be prophetic and filled with Biblical patterns no one cares to learn.

Becoming the Bride of Christ

Twenty plus years I have studied the seven churches. Every time I re-enter the teaching, I learn anew. God has called me to warn the American church God loves, will you hear what the Holy Spirit is saying, and repent and return to the entire word of God?

He was crucified upon a cross of wood, yet he created the hill upon which it stood. He is returning for his bride very soon.

In Christ's eternal service John Burns RLTW, 1-8-2022.

Special Operations Wounded Warriors

2016 was my official homecoming. The community I once served, was asking me to serve once more, but not before welcoming me home.

It had been twenty-three years since I returned from Mogadishu, Somalia injured. It had been a long time since I had toasted the men I lost, and brothers I never got to say goodbye to. This organization exists to find men like me. Brothers-in-arms who somehow got lost on the road after doing exactly what their creed requires. Somewhere along the way I had stopped Rangering. Or so I thought.

I was a United States Army Airborne Ranger. I spent five years in a Rifle Company in the 75th Ranger Regiment. I would dare to say the best Ranger rifle company the Regiment has ever seen. I was one bearing in the gears of Bravo Company that when in time, made the whole engine work. Bravo Company was home to me, and the men I served with are my family. The DNA that makes up our family, can never be manipulated. It is a blood covenant.

Rangers serve at the behest of the president. They are as close to tier one as any unit gets. While not always enjoying the budgets of other special operations units, no unit has been asked to do more for our country. And Bravo Company has led the way every time.

On Rio Hata in Panama, Bravo Company 3/75 lost SSG. Larry Bernard and Pfc. Roy Brown, with Bill Dunham and Patrick Kilgallen suffering injuries that still remind them each day of their sacrifice. These men are the reason I served.

I had the privilege of welcoming these men home from the hospital in 1990. I have remained a steadfast advocate for my brothers and my best friend in life served in their platoon in Panama. Paul Mercer is the greatest Ranger and best American I have ever met and called my friend.

I remained In B 3/75 for five years. I served in positions ranging from Mortar Section FDC Chief, Team Leader in a Rifle Platoon, Squad Leader of a Rifle Squad and culminating in my job in Somalia, Weapons Squad Leader, Third Platoon B 3/75 Rgr Regt. The greatest privilege the Lord Jesus Christ ever bestowed upon me was the privilege to lead Rangers in combat. Nothing since has kept my attention.

In Somalia I had an amazing group of men in my squad. My three machine gunners were all better than me at being a daily Ranger. Dominic Pilla, Chris Schlief, and Dave Ritchie are three amazing Americans. Dominic would die in Somalia leading with lead, and killing his killer. Chris Schlief was unwavering in Mogadishu, and the most brilliant man I have ever encountered. He has continued to serve our country in special operations and today he is A CSM in an SF Group. Dave Ritchie was my gunner on my vehicle on October 3, 1993. He is my hero. He was wounded early in the mission and continued to fight with an M16 after his Mg was disabled. Dave ended up leading our vehicle home when I was wounded near the front of the convoy for the third time. Dave was a Spec4 in Somalia. I had my gunner Clay Othic wounded seriously with the loss of his shooting arm. Lorenzo Ruiz took over the 50 caliber, and was fatally wounded taking over from Clay Othic. I was wounded once by gunfire early, and once by Shrapnel before I was hit the third time making my way back through the convoy toward my vehicle. That left a Spec4 in charge of my vehicle team, and the rear of the convoy. Dave Ritchie was able to lead them for two hours as we fought our way back to our base. Dave Ritchie would go on to serve in Task Force 160th as a CH 47 pilot for every year of the GWOT. He retired a CW4, and continues to serve his state as a pilot fighting forest fires in California. He is an American Special Operations hero.

Chad Fowles was an AG for Dave Ritchie and drove our vehicle. He somehow managed to not get hit in Somalia. God has a plan for Chad Fowles, and I pray SOWW helps him find it. Chad retired as a MSG with twenty years in the Army. Along for the ride on my vehicle was PFC Jason Dancy. He also managed to not get hit, but it does not diminish his contribution to the Regiment and Bravo Company lure. He fought like a Spartan on October 3, 1993. Reese Teakell was Chris Schlief's new ammo bearer in Somalia. His first deployment in Bravo Company was to Somalia. Reese went on to serve the Regiment after returning from Somalia in every position from team leader to squad leader to CSM of the Special Troops Battalion. He is today a CSM in a Brigade of the 82d Airborne division. Ed Kallman rounds out weapons Squad who fought on October 3, 1993. He was the driver for another vehicle and managed to not get wounded. I was privileged to lead these men in support of the Special Operations mission to Somalia. I intend to work tirelessly to bring these men home to SOWW and back together as a Ranger family.

I left the Army in 1995. I was a Platoon Sergeant in Vicenza, Italy. A final act of mercy from a loving God. I got to share with my platoon in Italy the lives of my squad, and their heroism in service to the Regiment and SOCCOM. I live every day for the chance to share my life and it's struggles with my Ranger brothers and SOWW is the platform that continues to make it possible.

As the country debates our nation's path forward, one thing that is undebatable. The true 1% of Americans that should be recognized are the 1% of Americans that have actually volunteered to defend the American life we enjoy on battlefields most Americans know not exist. When you break it down further, less than 1 tenth of 1% of those ever serve in a special mission unit. The freedom we all profess comes at a cost that continues to be paid for by the 1 tenth of 1% of Americans who get to call themselves the SOCCOM family. It is a family that can never be divided, and SOWW is the greatest mechanism for keeping the family recognized and together, as we embark on the next phase of our lives.

America has once again become apathetic to all things military. We can never surrender. If we surrender, this entire experiment of a government of the people, for the people, and by the people will perish from the earth.

SOWW exists to make sure America never forgets the lives led by Rangers, Seals, Operators, and Airmen, who continue to provide America with a blanket of protection. The freedom we enjoy is because of men who serve in SOCCOM. SOWW is the place where SOCCOM family reunions continue to occur.

I was privileged to meet a man I now can identify as my brother while attending a SOWW event in South Carolina. I was stepping out in extreme faith by attending this event. My Ranger brother, and survivor of Mogadishu, Dave Floyd had invited me to the annual SOWW hog hunt called Takin Bacon. I accepted and boy was God a gracious God. Not only did I connect with men I had served with, I got to meet an entire generation of special men who had now served our country in a protracted war with no end in sight. But one I will never forget. Eddie Oglesby was one of the dog handlers. I felt there was something more to Eddie so I struck up a conversation with him. Eddie had served our nation in Viet Nam as a Ranger in Papa Company 75th Infantry. He and I were DNA brothers, and we were meeting at SOWW. I sensed Eddie was experiencing his own sort of homecoming. SOWW was the mechanism by which Eddie and I connected, and we will be brothers who look forward to Takin Bacon every year. I miss Eddie every day. He taught me more about responsibility to my brothers than any shrink could ever hope to learn in twenty years of practice. SOWW did that for me and an old Ranger from Viet Nam who came home to a divided nation. Imagine the Rangers coming home now?

SOWW provides special men with the opportunity to share their experiences with people who will be able to show empathy rather than sympathy. The stories would never be understood by a public that has lost its sense of understanding toward freedom's high cost. Special Operations Wounded Warriors caters to the needs of men who have been wounded defending our ideals as Judeo-Christian Americans. Our creeds are our bond and promise to this nation. Our experiences in war are our bond to each other.

SOWW has put its money where its mouth is. Warriors from the SOCCOM community gather each year in March to fellowship, kill wild boar, and party like it's 1999. The place where this occurs cost money every year to lease. We at SOWW have been afforded the opportunity to purchase the property and make it a permanent destination throughout the year for men and families in our very small community who have borne the brunt of this protracted war on terror. It will never end, and our mission to our community will never end. Consider giving a monetary gift to further our mission from once a year to permanent status. The property along the river comes at a cost of three million dollars.

I know the Ranger community alone could raise that! This organization is limiting the damage to warriors in our community who need us to continue the family bonds on into eternity. We have borne the brunt of the freedom debt our country expects us to continue to pay. Please help us reach our goal.

Donations to our cause should be sent via www.sowwcharity.com. Please prayerfully consider helping our cause. It is our nations cause!

RLTW John Burns, He was crucified upon a Cross of wood yet he created the hill upon which it stood 6-9-2020.

A portion of the proceeds from the sale of every book will be donated to Special Operations Wounded Warriors in the name of Daniel D. Busch.

A portion of the proceeds will also go to Behind the Veil Ministries in the name of CW2 Aaron A. Weaver. My Ranger brother, an American hero, and a friend to all things Jesus Christ.

The rest of the proceeds will support Gold Star programs supported by the USSOCCOM community. We owe these family members continued support as they navigate this life without the brothers we served with.

Rangers Lead the Way!

Biography

John Burns is a staff writer at the Morgan County Today newspaper, the Chaplain of Special Operations Wounded Warriors non-profit, and the President of Behind the Veil Ministries Inc.

His Christian faith is the foundation for every aspect of his life. He is married to Susan C. Burns of Lancing, TN. He is blessed with four grown children; Sean, Andrew, Kasey, and Lisa. He also has eleven wonderful grandchildren.

His hobbies include; turkey hunting, hound dogs, hog hunting, beer tasting, coffee drinking, and studying the Bible every day.

His ministry to the special operations community was born out of his desire to serve the community that gave him so much in life.

"The men who came before me were giants. They led the way and ensured we would give it one hell of a go. I have so many to thank. The only way I know how is to serve them tirelessly so we can all fellowship forever on the other side of glory."

The road goes on forever, and the party never ends…

He was crucified upon a cross of wood yet he created the hill upon which it stood.

Printed in Great Britain
by Amazon